Jung Uncorked
Book Two

Marie-Louise von Franz, Honorary Patron

**Studies in Jungian Psychology
by Jungian Analysts**

Daryl Sharp, General Editor

JUNG UNCORKED

Rare Vintages from the Cellar
Of Analytical Psychology

BOOK TWO

Decanted with commentaries by
DARYL SHARP

For those in search of meaning

Library and Archives Canada Cataloguing in Publication

Sharp, Daryl, 1936-
  Jung Uncorked: rare vintages from the cellar of
  analytical psychology / Daryl Sharp.

(Studies in Jungian psychology by Jungian analysts; 120, 121)

Includes bibliographical references and index.

ISBN 978-1-894574-21-1 (bk. 1)
ISBN 978-1-894574-22-8 (bk. 2)

1.   Jungian psychology. I. Title. II. Series.

BF173.S517 2008   150.19'54   C2007-905580-X

INNER CITY BOOKS
Box 1271, Station Q, Toronto, ON M4T 2P4, Canada

Telephone (416) 927-0355 / Fax (416) 924-1814

Toll-free (Canada and U.S.): Tel 1-888-927-0355 / Fax 1-888-924-1814

Web site: www.innercitybooks.net.
E-mail: booksales@innercitybooks.net

Honorary Patron: Marie-Louise von Franz.
Publisher and General Editor: Daryl Sharp.
Senior Editor: Victoria Cowan.
Office Manager: Scott Milligen.

INNER CITY BOOKS was founded in 1980 to promote the
understanding and practical application of the work of C.G. Jung.

Printed and bound in Canada by Thistle Printing Ltd.

CONTENTS

See next page for Book Two

BOOK TWO:

See final pages for descriptions of other titles in this Series

But now the days are short,
I'm in the autumn of the year,
And now I think of my life
as vintage wine from fine old kegs.
From the brim to the dregs,
it pours sweet and clear,
It was a very good year.

—Frank Sinatra, *It Was a Very Good Year*

.

Life is short. If you don't wake up,
you might miss it.

—*Prof. Adam Brillig (ret.)*

Everything young grows old, all beauty fades, all heat cools, all
brightness dims, and every truth becomes stale and trite. . . .
A truth is valid in the end only if it suffers change and bears new
witness in new images, in new tongues, like a new wine that is put
into new bottles.

—*C.G. Jung, Symbols of Transformation.*

We need more psychology.
We need more understanding of human nature,
because the only real danger that exists is man himself.
He is the great danger,
and we are pitifully unaware of it.
—C.G. Jung, "The 'Face to Face' Interview," 1959.

Preface

C.G. Jung died in 1961 at the age of 86, but his legacy lives on, mightily. His writings are like fine, full-bodied wines—they mature with age, as do we all if we pay sufficient attention to ourselves.

Jung Uncorked celebrates Jung. It presents spirited passages in his *Collected Works* (CW) together with my experiential commentaries on their psychological significance and contemporary relevance. Of course the selections here are just the tip of the wine cellar, so to speak, that is Jung's legacy and, by extension, the backdrop to the attitude toward the psyche that generally informs the modern practice of analytical psychology.

Some of the material here may be familiar to readers from other contexts. That is to be welcomed. Consider that we all come back to psychological writings anew, according to where we are on our spiral path of self-understanding. For myself, after thirty years practicing as a Jungian analyst, and editing and publishing books by many colleagues, I am still struck by Jung's all-encompassing wisdom and insights into the workings of the human psyche. Indeed, although I am quite familiar with all the essays in his *Collected Works,* wherever I open a volume it is as if I had never read it before. My knees become weak and I am inspirited anew.

Jung Uncorked is published in two volumes. In order to cover Jung's wide range of interests, the chapters in the two Books deal with one essay from each volume of the *Collected Works,* sequentially from CW 1 to CW 18. Book One explicates and comments on essays from CW volumes 1-9i. Book Two does the same with CW volumes 9ii to 18.

Since Book One contains more explanations of Jung's basic concepts, it is advisable to read it before Book Two.

9ii
The Syzygy: Anima and Animus
(from *Aion,* CW 9ii; vintage 1951)

The autonomy of the collective unconscious expresses itself in the figures of anima and animus. They personify those of its contents, which, when withdrawn from projection, can be integrated into consciousness. To this extent, both figures represent *functions* which filter the contents of the unconscious through to the conscious mind. . . . Though the effects of anima and animus can be made conscious, they themselves are factors transcending consciousness and beyond the reach of perception and volition. Hence they remain autonomous despite the integration of their contents, and for this reason they should be borne constantly in mind.[1]

Syzygy, what a strange name. What language is it? You won't find it in many English dictionaries. What could it mean, and why did Jung choose such an arcane term to describe the connection between the contrasexual archetypes?

Jung does not enlighten us in this essay with answers to such questions. But Edward F. Edinger, at the beginning of his masterful commentary on *Aion,* does:

[Syzygy] means pair or couple. The pairs of aions that the Gnostic god emanated were called syzygies, but the original meaning of the word was "to yoke together." It is derived from two different stems: "syn" [Greek] meaning with, and "zygon" meaning yoke or the cross-bar of a harness. The longitudinal bar of the harness is connected to the wagon as illustrated [Figure 1], and the cross bar is called the zygon. The necks of the horses slip into the two loops of the zygon. The zygon or the syzygy literally means the pair of horses that are yoked together in a single harness.[2]

---

[1] "The Syzygy: Anima and Animus," *Aion,* CW 9ii, par. 40.
[2] *The Aion Lectures: Exploring the Self in C.G. Jung's* Aion, p. 28.

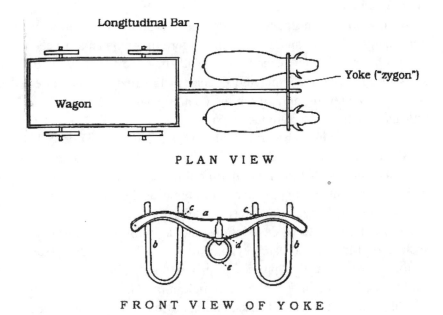

PLAN VIEW

FRONT VIEW OF YOKE

Figure 1. Syzygy.

Anima and animus, then, in Jung's formulation, are yoked together in the human psyche. What does this mean? It means they are fatefully conjoined, which may manifest in either attraction or enmity, or both.

What a novel concept to us moderns, the notion of a feminine personality in a man and a masculine figure in a woman's psyche. But it was gospel to the ancients, especially the Gnostics, a group of sects that flourished among the Greeks in the first few centuries A.D. They believed implicitly in the contrasexual nature of all individuals, which together produced Truth.

Before discussing the syzygy, Jung spends some pages describing the lineaments of the shadow and the difficulties in apprehending it. He implies that the assimilation of the shadow is the apprentice-work, but integrating the anima or animus is the master-work.

Let us look closely at the two separately.

Jung had a number of descriptions and definitions of the anima, such as soul-image and "archetype of life itself,"[3] but in this essay he focuses on her as the "projection-making factor" in a man's psyche. She saves a man from being a stick-in-the-mud, prods him to adventure and the taking of risks, alternately enlivens and maddens him. And everything she does to him inside is reflected and amplified, through projection, in his activities and relationships in the outside world.

Psychologically the anima is both an archetype, a collective primordial image, and on the personal level a complex, functioning in a man as his soul. When a man is full of life he is "animated." The man with no connection to his inner woman feels dull and listless. Nowadays we call this depression, but the experience is not new. For thousands of years, among so-called primitive peoples, this state of being has been known as loss of soul.

A man's anima complex is initially determined by his experience of his personal mother or closest female caregiver. It is later modi-

---

[3] "Archetypes of the Collective Unconscious," *The Archetypes and the Collective Unconscious,* CW 9i, par. 66.

fied through contact with other women—friends, lovers, relatives, teachers—but the experience of the personal mother is so powerful and long-lasting that a man is naturally attracted to those women who are much like her—or, as often happens, her direct opposite. That is to say, he may yearn for what he has known, or seek to escape it at all costs.

A man who is unconscious of his feminine side is apt to see that aspect of himself, whatever its characteristics may be, in an actual woman. This happens via projection and is commonly experienced as falling in love, or, conversely, as intense dislike. A man may also project his anima onto another man, in love or hate, though in practice this is often difficult to distinguish from the projection of the man's shadow.

The man unrelated to his inner woman also tends to be moody, sometimes gentle and sentimental but prone to sudden rage and violence. Analysts call this being anima-possessed. By paying attention to his moods and emotional reactions—objectifying and personifying them—a man can come into possession of his soul rather than be possessed by it. As with any complex, the negative influence of the anima is reduced by establishing a conscious relationship with it.

Jung distinguished four broad stages of the anima in the course of a man's psychological development. He personified these, according to classical stages of eroticism, as Eve, Helen, Mary and Sophia.[4]

In the first stage, Eve, the man's anima is completely tied up with the mother—not necessarily his personal mother, but the image of woman as safe haven, faithful provider of nourishment, security and love. The man with an anima of this type cannot function well without a vital connection to a woman and is easy prey to being controlled by her. He frequently suffers impotence or has no

---

[4] "The Psychology of the Transference," *The Practice of Psychotherapy,* CW 16, par. 361; see also Marie-Louise von Franz, "The Process of Individuation," in C.G. Jung and von Franz, eds., *Man and His Symbols,* pp. 185f.

sexual desire at all.

In the second stage, personified in the historical figure of Helen of Troy, the anima is a collective sexual image. She is Marlene Dietrich, Marilyn Monroe, Tina Turner, Madonna, all rolled up into one. The man under her spell is often a Don Juan who engages in repeated sexual adventures. These will invariably be short-lived, for two reasons: 1) he has a fickle heart—his feelings are whimsical and often gone in the morning—and 2) no real woman can live up to the expectations that go with this unconscious, ideal image.

The third stage of the anima is Mary. It manifests in religious feelings and a capacity for genuine friendship with women. The man with an anima of this kind is able to see a woman as she is, independent of his own needs. His sexuality is integrated into his life, not an autonomous function that drives him. He can differentiate between love and lust. He is capable of lasting relationships because he can tell the difference between the object of his desire and his inner image of woman.

In the fourth stage, as Sophia (called Wisdom in the Bible), a man's anima functions as a guide to the inner life, mediating to consciousness the contents of the unconscious. Sophia is behind the need to grapple with the grand philosophical issues, the search for meaning. She is Beatrice in Dante's *Inferno,* and the creative muse in any artist's life. She is a natural mate for the archetypal "wise old man" in the male psyche. The sexuality of a man at this stage incorporates a spiritual dimension.

Theoretically, a man's anima development proceeds through these stages as he grows older and assimilates his experiences of the opposite sex. When the possibilities of one stage have been exhausted—which is to say, when adaptation to oneself and outer circumstances requires it—the psyche stimulates the move to the next stage.

In fact, the transition from one stage to another seldom happens without a struggle, for the psyche not only promotes and supports growth, it is also, paradoxically, conservative and loath to give up what it knows. Hence a psychological crisis is commonly precipitated when there is a pressing need for a man to move from one stage to the next.

For that matter, a man may have periodic contact with any number of anima images, at any time of life, depending on what is required to compensate the current dominant conscious attitude. The reality is that psychologically men live in a harem. Any man may observe this for himself by paying close attention to his dreams and fantasies. His soul-image appears in many different forms, as myriad as the expressions of an actual woman's femininity.

In subhuman guise, the anima may manifest as snake, toad, cat or bird; or on a slightly higher level as nixie, pixie, mermaid. In human form—to mention only a few personifications modeled on goddesses in Greek mythology—the anima may appear as Hera, consort and queen; Demeter/Persephone, the mother-daughter team; Aphrodite, the lover; Pallas Athene, carrier of culture and protectress of heroes; Artemis, the stand-offish huntress; and Hecate, ruler in the netherworld of magic.

The assimilation of a particular anima-image results in its death, so to speak. That is to say, as one personification of the anima is consciously understood, it is supplanted by another. Anima development in a man is thus a continuous process of death and rebirth. An overview of this process is very important in surviving the transition stage between one anima-image and the next. Just as no real woman relishes being discarded for another, so no anima figure willingly takes second place to her upstart rival. In this regard, as in so much else involved in a person's psychological development, the good is the enemy of the better. To have contact with your inner woman at all is a blessing; to be tied to one that holds you back can be fatal.

While the old soul-mate clamors for the attention that now, in order for the man to move on, is demanded by and due to the new one, the man is often assailed by conflicting desires. The struggle is not just an inner, metaphorical one; it also involves his lived relationships. The resultant suffering and inner turmoil, the tension and sleepless nights, are comparable to what occurs in any conflict situation.

The dominant anima-image that must be supplanted is often characterized in fairy tales as the false bride, while the new one is called the true bride. The essential difference between the two is captured in Marie-Louise von Franz's observation: "The truth of yesterday must be set aside for what is *now* the truth of one's own psychic life."[5]

True and false brides don't come labeled, and so are difficult to recognize. Much depends on a man's age, his position in life and how much work he has done on himself—particularly the extent to which he has already differentiated his soul-image from the other complexes teeming in his psyche.

Theoretically, there are two basic types of false bride. One is an anima figure—or an actual woman—who leads a man into the fantasy realm, away from timely responsibilities in the outside world. The other is an inner voice—or again a real woman—that would tie a man to his persona when his real task is to turn inward, to find out what is behind the face he shows others.

The first type is commonly associated with the idealistic, and age-appropriate, attitudes of a younger man: the disinclination to compromise, a rigid response to the reality of everyday life. The second type of false bride is often associated with regressive tendencies in later life, evident in those who make feverish efforts to mask their age or reclaim their lost youth through younger companions, fitness regimes, face lifts, hair transplants and so on.

There is no hard and fast rule, however. An older man with too much unlived life may have to descend into the whore's cellar, so to speak, as part of his individuation process. The younger man with no ideals may be forced to develop some. Such things are the daily concerns of analysis.

As happens with any psychological content, the bride of either

---

[5] *Redemption Motifs in Fairytales,* p. 85.

type, when not recognized as an inner reality, appears in the outside world through projection. If a man's anima is lonely and desperate for attention, he will tend to fall in love with dependent women who demand all his time and energy. The man with a mother-bound anima will get tied up with women who want to take care of him. The man not living up to his potential will fall for women who goad him on. In short, whatever qualities a man does not recognize in himself—shadow, anima, whatever—will confront him in real life. Outer reflects inner; that is the general rule. If there are any psychological rules that are valid always and everywhere, that is one of them.

The seductive lure of the false bride manifests in outer life not only as a tie to an unsuitable woman, but also as the wrong choice in a conflict situation. This is due to the regressive tendencies of the unconscious. Each new stage of development, each foothold on an increase in consciousness, must be wrested anew from the dragon-like grip of the past. This kind of work on oneself is called by Jung *contra naturam,* against nature. That is because nature is essentially conservative and unconscious. There is a lot to be said for the natural mind and the healthy instincts that go with it, but not much in terms of consciousness.

As the mediating function between the ego and the unconscious, the anima is complementary to the persona and stands in a compensatory relationship to it. That is to say, all those qualities absent from the outer attitude will be found in the inner. Jung gives the example of a tyrant tormented by bad dreams and gloomy forebodings:

> Outwardly ruthless, harsh, and unapproachable, he jumps inwardly at every shadow, is at the mercy of every mood, as though he were the feeblest and most impressionable of men. Thus his anima contains all those fallible human qualities his persona lacks.[6]

Similarly, when a man identifies with his persona, he is in effect

---

[6] "Definitions," *Psychological Types,* CW 6, par. 804.

possessed by the anima, with all the attendant symptoms.

> Identity . . . with the persona automatically leads to an unconscious identity with the anima because, when the ego is not differentiated from the persona, it can have no conscious relation to the unconscious processes. Consequently it *is* these processes, it is identical with them. Anyone who is himself his outward role will infallibly succumb to the inner processes; he will either frustrate his outward role by absolute inner necessity or else reduce it to absurdity, by a process of *enantiodromia*. . . . He can no longer keep to his individual way, and his life runs into one deadlock after another. Moreover, the anima is inevitably projected upon a real object, with which he gets into a relation of almost total dependence.[7]

Thus it is essential for a man to distinguish between who he is and who he appears to be. Symptomatically, in fact, there is no significant difference between persona identification and anima possession; both are indications of unconsciousness.

Let us turn now to the animus.

A woman's inner image of men is strongly colored by her experience of the personal father. Just as a man is apt to marry his mother, so to speak, so a woman is inclined to favor a man psychologically like her father; or, again, his opposite.

Whereas the anima in a man functions as his soul, a woman's animus is more like an unconscious mind. It manifests negatively in fixed ideas, unconscious assumptions and conventional opinions that may be generally right but just beside the point in a particular situation. A woman unconscious of her masculine side tends to be highly opinionated and critical—animus-possessed. This kind of woman proverbially wears the pants; she rules the roost—or tries to. The men attracted to her may be driven to distraction by her whims, coldly emasculated, while she herself wears a mask of indifference to cover her insecurity.

A woman's animus becomes a helpful psychological factor only

---

[7] Ibid., par. 807. *Enantiodromia* refers to the emergence of the unconscious opposite in the course of time.

when she can tell the difference between "him" and herself. While a man's task in assimilating the anima involves discovering his true feelings, a woman must constantly question her collective ideas and opinions, measuring these against what *she* really thinks. If she does so, in time the animus can become a valuable inner companion who endows her with qualities of enterprise, courage, objectivity and spiritual wisdom.

Jung describes four stages of animus development in a woman, similar to those of the anima in a man. He first appears in dreams and fantasy as the embodiment of physical power, for instance an athlete or muscle man, a Samson or James Bond. This corresponds to the anima as Eve. For a woman with such an animus a man is simply a stud; he exists to give her physical satisfaction, protection and healthy babies.

In the second stage, analogous to the anima as Helen, the animus possesses initiative and the capacity for planned action. He is behind a woman's desire for independence and a career of her own. However, a woman with an animus of this type still relates to a man on a collective level: he is the generic husband-father, the man around the house whose primary role is to provide shelter and support for his family—Mr. Do-All, Mr. Fix-It, with no life of his own.

In the next stage, corresponding to the anima as Mary, the animus is the Word, often personified in dreams as a professor, clergyman or some other authoritarian figure. A woman with such an animus has a great respect for traditional learning; she is capable of sustained creative work and welcomes the opportunity to exercise her mind. She is able to relate to a man on an individual level, as lover rather than husband or father, and she ponders her own elusive identity.

In the fourth stage, the animus is the incarnation of spiritual meaning—a Mahatma Gandhi, Martin Luther King or Dalai Lama. On this highest level, like the anima as Sophia, the animus mediates between a woman's conscious mind and the unconscious. In mythology he appears as Hermes, messenger of the gods; or in female guise as Iris, goddess of the rainbow, connecting heaven and earth; in dreams he is a helpful guide. Sexuality for such a woman is imbued with spiritual significance.

Any of these aspects of the animus can be projected onto a man, who will be expected to live up to the projected image—or else. As mentioned earlier, the same is true of the anima. So in any relationship between a man and a woman there are at least four personalities involved, as shown in the diagram below.[8]

The most positive aspects of a woman's animus manifest when she has assimilated it, consciously integrated it. Jung writes:

> Just as the anima becomes, through integration, the Eros of consciousness, so the animus becomes a Logos; and in the same way that the anima gives relationship and relatedness to a man's consciousness, the animus gives to woman's consciousness a capacity for reflection, deliberation, and self-knowledge.[9]

Theoretically, there is no difference between an unconscious man and a woman's tyrannical animus. The implication is that an unconscious man can be coerced into being or doing whatever a woman wants. But it's just as true the other way around: unconscious women are easily seduced into becoming a reflection of a man's anima. In relationships there are no innocent victims.

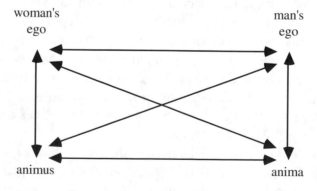

$$\text{woman's ego} \qquad \text{man's ego}$$

animus   anima

---

[8] Adapted from Jung's "cross-cousin" drawing in "The Psychology of the Transference," *The Practice of Psychotherapy*, CW 16, par. 422.

[9] "The Syzygy: Anima and Animus," *Aion*, CW 9ii, par. 33.

The more differentiated a woman is in her own femininity, the more able she is to reject whatever unsuitable role is projected onto her by a man. This forces the man back on himself. If he has the capacity for self-examination and insight, he may discover in himself the basis for false expectations. Failing inner resources on either side, there is only rancor and animosity.

Analogous to the true and false anima-brides discussed above, there are true and false bridegrooms. The latter may manifest as a woman's feelings of worthlessness and despair, and in her outer life as a compulsive tie to, say, an authoritarian father figure or an abusive partner. The true bridegroom gives her confidence in herself, encourages her endeavors and is interested in her mind as well as her body.

In the best of all possible worlds, the true bridegroom finds his mate in the true bride, and vice versa. Of course, this is no guarantee that they will live happily ever after. No matter how individuated one is, no matter how much one has worked on oneself, projection and conflict in relationships are always possible, if not inevitable. But that is no bad thing; we are human, after all, and such things keep us on our toes.

Intimate relationships are fraught with difficulty. There are any number of landmines to be negotiated before two people feel comfortable with each other; more when they become sexually involved, and more again if and when they live together. On top of projection and identification, there are each other's personal complexes and typological differences. In truth, the very things that brought them together in the first place are just as likely to drive them apart.

Assuming that most relationships begin with mutual good will, why do so many end in acrimony? There are probably as many answers to this as there are couples who split up, but in terms of a common pattern, typology certainly plays a major role.[10]

The yoking together of anima and animus is almost always full of animosity, which is to say, loaded with emotion. Jung puts it quite graphically:

> When animus and anima meet, the animus draws his sword of power and the anima ejects her poison of illusion and seduction.[11]

How, then, is one to work on a relationship? Now, I am no expert, having burned as many bridges as I have built, but I have some suggestions.

You work on a relationship by shutting your mouth when you are ready to explode; by not inflicting your affect on the other person; by quietly leaving the battlefield and tearing your hair out; by asking yourself—not your partner—what complex in you was activated, and to what end. The proper question is not, "Why is she doing that to me?" or "Who does he think he is?" but rather, "Why am I reacting in this way?—Who do *I* think he or she is?" And more: "What does this say about my psychology? What can I do about it?" Instead of accusing the other person of driving you crazy, you say to yourself, "I feel I'm being driven crazy—where, or who, in me is that coming from?" It also helps to personify the animus or anima; give him or her a name and have a dialogue with that person. In this way you bring it all home, where it belongs.

That is how, over time, you establish a container, a personal temenos, a safe haven independent of your mate or anyone else.

It is true that a strong emotion sometimes needs to be expressed, because it comes not from a complex but from genuine feeling. There is a fine line between the two, and it is extremely difficult to tell one from the other without a container. But when you can tell the difference you can speak from the heart.

Working on a relationship involves keeping your mood to your-

---

[10] See *Jung Uncorked,* Book One, chap. 6, "The Type Problem" and chap. 7, "The Problem of the Attitude-Type."

[11] "The Syzygy: Anima and Animus," *Aion,* CW 9ii, par. 30.

self and examining it. You neither bottle up the emotion nor allow it to poison the air. The merit in this approach is that it throws us back entirely on our experience of ourselves. It is foolish to imagine we can change the person who seems to be the cause of our heart-ache. But with the proper container we can change ourselves and our reactions.

It used to be thought that "letting it all hang out" was the thing to do. But that is merely allowing the complex to take over. The trick is to get some distance from the complex, objectify it, take a stand toward it. You can't do this if you identify with it, if you can't tell the difference between yourself and the emotion that grabs you by the throat when a complex is active. And you can't do it without a container.

Those who think that talking about a relationship will help it get better put the cart before the horse. Work on yourself and a good relationship will follow. You can either accept who you are and find a relationship that fits, or twist yourself out of shape and get what you deserve.

The endless blather that takes place between two complexed people solves nothing. It is a waste of time and energy and as often as not actually makes the situation worse. It is worth saying again:

> When animus and anima meet, the animus draws his sword of power and the anima ejects her poison of illusion and seduction.[12]

Of course, the meeting between anima and animus is not always negative. In the beginning, at least, the two are just as likely to be starry-eyed lovers. Later, when reality sets in and the bloom is off the rose, they may even become fast friends. But the major battles in close relationships occur because the man has not withdrawn his anima projection on the woman, and/or the woman still projects her animus onto the man.

We may understand this intellectually, but when someone we love does not behave according to the image we have of him or her,

---

[12] Ibid.

all hell breaks loose. We are instantly complexed. Our emotions do not coincide with what is in our heads or hearts. Our reactions run the gamut between outright violence, seething anger, self-righteousness and grieved silence, depending on our psychology. Whatever the immediate reaction, it is bound to happen again unless we reflect on what is behind it.

I give you George, successful advertising executive in his mid-forties, happily married with three grown sons. He came to see me because he was obsessed with a young woman he barely knew. In our third session together he showed me a letter he had written her:

Dear Ms. Cotton Pants,

It is close to midnight, an ungodly hour to exorcise demons, but I have to declare myself. I have torn myself away from Hitchcock movies on the television to tell you that I am besotted with you.

You may not remember me. Well, that's no surprise. You wouldn't notice me in a crowd, and we only brushed shoulders once at a concert hall some months ago. I saw the moon in your eyes and I was immediately smitten, don't ask me why. I tracked you down and I have stalked you ever since. Oh, don't be afraid, I mean you no harm.

Now, I don't wish to be importunate, but I must see you in order to stay sane. Perhaps we can meet some day for coffee and a bagel. Please say yes, it would mean so much to me. I can be reached at Butterfield 9062, any time of day or night. Just ask for George. Please help! I am desperately in love with you.

"I haven't sent it," said George, tearfully. "I wanted to talk to you first." He showed me a picture of a cute seventeen-year-old.

Confidentiality prevents me from divulging details of our subsequent conversations, but I can say that George was relieved to hear that his plight was not unique and that he was not certifiably crazy. He gladly absorbed what I told him about the phenomenon of projection and he was open to the possibility of a feminine side of himself that he saw in "Ms. Cotton Pants," a fanciful moniker he associated with a teenage girlfriend, a cheerleader who brazenly flashed her undies in public but locked knees in private. He also confessed that when watching movies he often imagined her in the role of the heroine. Well, it was not long before George stopped obsessing about Ms. Cotton Pants and turned his attention to his wife.

Jung ends this essay on the syzygy by emphasizing the disruptive power of anima and animus as long as they remain unconscious and projected:

> Those who do not see them are in their hands, just as a typhus epidemic flourishes best when its source is undiscovered. . . . What we can discover about them from the conscious side is so slight as to be almost imperceptible. It is only when we throw light into the dark depths of the psyche and explore the strange and tortured paths of human fate that it gradually becomes clear to us how immense is the influence wielded by these two factors that complement our conscious life.[13]

Consider this: zoologists have observed that among a certain breed of fish, the *cichlidae,* a male can combine sex with aggression, but not sex and fear. In the female, sex and fear can be combined, but not aggression and sex. Jung's analyst-colleague Marie-Louise von Franz sees this little-known fact as a psychological verity applicable to the behavior of humans, stating, "There you have the animus-anima problem in a nutshell."[14] Now, this sounds like an outlandish proposition, for it implies that a woman may mate with a man she is afraid of, but a man is rendered impotent by an aggressive woman.

Well, I wouldn't know about that. All I know for sure is that in the best of loving circumstances there is a satisfying congruence between giving oneself and being taken.

---

[13] Ibid., par. 41.

[14] Von Franz, *The Problem of the Puer Aeternus,* p. 173.

10
A Psychological View of Conscience
(from *Civilization in Transition,* CW 10; vintage 1958)

Conscience—no matter on what it is based—commands the individual to obey his inner voice even at the risk of going astray.[15]

There is scarcely any other psychic phenomenon that shows the polarity of the psyche in a clearer light than conscience. Its undoubted dynamism, in order to be understood at all, can only be explained in terms of energy, that is, as a potential based on opposites. Conscience brings these ever-present and necessary opposites to conscious perception. It would be a great mistake to suppose that one could ever get rid of this polarity, for it is an essential element in the psychic structure.[16]

In this essay Jung is at great pains to differentiate conscience as a personal psychic function *(ethos/*ethics) from conscience based on a collective moral code *(mores/*morality)—for instance the Ten Commandments, or what is otherwise historically or culturally sanctioned in a given society.

This is no easy task, especially since the notion of the so-called superego was introduced by Freud into our psychological vocabulary more than a hundred years ago. Jung points out that according to Freud's definition the superego is not a natural and inherited part of the psyche's structure, but rather the consciously acquired stock of traditional customs, a patriarchal legacy consistent with what is acceptable in a particular culture. In this essay Jung sets out to illustrate the inadequacy of that view as an explanation of our attitudes and behavior.

---

[15] "A Psychological View of Conscience," *Civilization in Transition,* CW 10, par. 841.
[16] Ibid., par. 844.

What is conscience and how does it manifest? To begin with, note that the word itself comes from the Latin *conscientia,* meaning a special form of knowledge or consciousness. From that, Jung moves to argue that conscience is an autonomous psychic factor, in other words, an unconscious function which properly does not depend on social factors. Now, this was—and to a great extent still is—a radical notion, but Jung never shrank from expressing radical ideas. Like any empirical scientist, he based his views on facts as he knew and experienced them.

Perhaps we have all known the uncomfortable thought or feeling that arises in us when we have said or done something that goes "against the grain." But what is "the grain"? Is it what other people say is okay, or is it some core value in ourselves that is abrogated? Or indeed, is it, as some believe, the *vox dei,* the guiding voice of God? Tough questions. Jung devotes a few hundred words to acknowledging that the belief in God's involvement is a psychological truth before dismissing it as an unworkable, unsatisfactory proposition, for God (Yahweh) is from all accounts himself morally ambivalent. And get this:

> Only unconscious and wholly uncritical people can imagine it possible to abide in a permanent state of moral goodness. But because most people are devoid of self-criticism, permanent self-deception is the rule.[17]

Is there a good conscience and a bad conscience—or only a conscience that kicks in when you do or think something "wrong"? If a man makes love to another man's wife, will he be punished by his conscience? Will she? And what form will their punishment, if any, take? But what if their love is felt by both to be "right," true to their process of individuation? Who then would be judge and executioner? If you pad your expense account, do you feel a "twinge of conscience"? If so, who or what is behind that twinge?

Jung delves into these questions so cogently that the head spins

---

[17] Ibid., par. 843.

as the idea of a functional superego is thoroughly and rationally demolished as a patriarchal legacy of little help to those suffering from conflicts of duty—that is, between two decisions equally "moral." In this category fall actions or activities that would be good for others, and those that are good only for oneself. In court trials, say, should a judge's decision be based on conventional wisdom, the moral code, or what he can personally live with? Such dilemmas pit *mores* against *ethos*. We are all influenced by our unconscious biases, also known as complexes. In other words, objectivity is a delusion fostered by the so-called Enlightenment and pervasive psychological ignorance.

In short, Jung champions an inner voice that tells us what is acceptable to us personally—an inner truth or *ethos* that must trump *mores,* collective moral standards, lest the personality become inauthentic. In the process of doing this he underscores the difference between collective moral precepts and a sense of what is ethically acceptable to our individual essence.

So what about this so-called ethical "inner voice"? Where does it come from and why is it to be trusted? Jung asks:

> Where does the true and authentic conscience, which rises above the moral code and refuses to submit to its dictate, get its justification from? What gives it the courage to assume that it is not a false conscience, a self-deception?[18]

Fair questions indeed, and Jung has convincing answers. For a start, there is the concept of the archetypes of the collective unconscious. Recall that the archetype is a pattern of behavior that has always existed. As a biological phenomenon it is morally indifferent but possesses a powerful dynamism by means of which it can profoundly influence human behavior. Archetypal images impress, influence and fascinate us. With this in mind, Jung writes that "conscience is a manifestation of *mana,* of the 'extraordinarily powerful,' a quality which is the especial peculiarity of archetypal

---

[18] Ibid., par. 838.

ideas."[19] Well, no wonder it takes unusual courage or unshakable faith for a person to follow the dictates of his or her own conscience (as opposed to a collective code). It is interesting to compare this with von Franz's comments on "the instinct of truth":

> One reacts rightly without knowing why, it flows through one and one does the right thing. . . . With the help of the instinct of truth, life goes on as a meaningful flow, as a manifestation of the Self.[20]

Jung goes on then to link the experience of conscience with the so-called psychoid archetype, synchronicity and the transcendent function (the *tertium non datur,* or third not logically given, which hopefully manifests if one holds the tension between the opposites long enough). This is admittedly a conceptual stretch, hard to follow even for a thinking type, but here are some of Jung's observations:

> The reduction of the act of conscience to a collision with the archetype is, by and large, a tenable explanation. On the other hand we must admit that the *psychoid* archetype, that is, its irrepresentable and unconscious essence, is not just a postulate only, but possesses qualities of a parapsychological nature which I have grouped together under the term "synchronicity" [= the meaningful conjunction in time of inner and outer phenomena].[21].

> As with all archetypal phenomena, the synchronicity factor must be taken into account in considering conscience. For although the voice of genuine conscience (and not just the recollection of the moral code) may make itself heard in the context of an archetypal situation, it is by no means certain that the reason for this is always a subjective moral reaction.[22]

---

[19] Ibid., par. 845. *Mana* is, a Melanesian word referring to the bewitching or numinous quality in gods and sacred objects.

[20] *Alchemy: An Introduction to the Symbolism and the Psychology,* pp. 172f.; see also *Jung Uncorked,* Book One, pp. 33f.

[21] "A Psychological View of Conscience," *Civilization in Transition,* CW 10, par. 849.

[22] Ibid., par. 850.

Conscience, in ordinary usage, refers to consciousness of a factor which in the case of a "good conscience" affirms that a decision or an act accords with collective morality and, if it does not, condemns it as "immoral." To this Jung counters:

> Distinct from this is the ethical form of conscience, which appears when two decisions or ways of acting, both affirmed to be moral and therefore regarded as "duties," collide with one another. In these cases, not foreseen by the moral code because they are mostly very individual, a judgment is required which cannot properly be called "moral" or in accord with custom. . . . The deciding factor appears to be something else: it proceeds not from the traditional moral code but from the unconscious foundation of the personality.[23]

When you reflect on issues having to do with conscience, there is no way to avoid dealing with the shadow. The other side of what we do and think is always there. You love your wife, but holy mackerel, your shadow does fancy that dolly you met in the gym. And on the other side of the fence, "Hey! What buns! I'd like to have him at the cottage for a weekend." You needn't feel ashamed about that; it is instinctive. You might have a bad conscience if you go to bed with that person, and she might too, but that's another story. Let us try not to confuse archetypes with instincts, though it is often difficult to distinguish between the two. I hold on to an understanding that instincts refer to physiological facts, and archetypes have to do with psychological phenomena.[24] All the same, there is undeniably an intertwining which Jung subsumes in his concept of the psychoid archetype.[25]

Although we don't know what motivated Jung to express his views on the topic of conscience, we do know that he had a long-standing extramarital relationship with his analyst-colleague Toni Woolf. We may dare to wonder if this clouded his judgment or en-

---

[23] Ibid., par. 856.

[24] See *Jung Uncorked,* Book One, pp. 18ff.

[25] For a fuller exposition, see Sparks, *At the Heart of Matter,* pp. 71ff.

hanced it. As an incurable romantic, I am inclined to believe the latter, and apparently his wife Emma did too.[26]

Jung ends his thoughts, or at least this essay, as follows:

> The concept and phenomenon of conscience thus contains, when seen in a psychological light, two different factors: on the one hand a recollection of, and admonition by, the *mores;* on the other, a conflict of duty and its solution through the creation of a third standpoint. The first is the moral, and the second the ethical, aspect of conscience.[27]

"Good and evil in Analytical Psychology"
(from *Civilization in Transition,* CW 10; vintage 1959)

From Jung's reflections on conscience to his thoughts on good and evil is not a big step, which is perhaps why the editors of the *Collected Works* put these essays in the same volume, this one after the one on conscience—and why I include it here.

Jung begins by noting his difficulties when discussing the problem of good and evil with philosophers and theologians:

> I have the impression that they are not talking about the thing itself, but only about words, about the concepts which denote or refer to it. We allow ourselves so easily to be deluded by words, we substitute words for the whole of reality. . . . When someone speaks of good or evil, it is of what *he* calls good or evil, or what *he* feels as good or evil. Then he speaks about it with great assurance, not knowing whether it really is so or whether what he calls good or evil really corresponds to the facts. Perhaps the speaker's view of the world is not in keeping with the real facts at all, so that an inner, subjective picture is substituted for objectivity.[28]

Good and evil, insists Jung, are in themselves principles, not

---

[26] See Barbara Hannah, *Jung: His Life and Work, A Biographical Memoir,* pp. 117ff.

[27] Ibid., par. 857.

[28] "Good and Evil in Analytical Psychology," *Civilization in Transition,* CW 10, par. 858.

facts, and their deeper qualities are in reality unknown to us. Furthermore, whether something is experienced as evil and sinful or good and moral depends on our subjective judgment and personal value system: Who knows for sure that what seems to him to be evil will not result in good, and vice versa?

> Where do we get this belief, this apparent certainty, that we know what is good and what is bad? "Ye shall be as gods, knowing good and evil." Only the gods know, not us. This is profoundly true in psychology. If you take the attitude: "This thing may be very bad— but on the other hand it may not," then you have a chance of doing the right thing. But if you already know in advance you are behaving as if you were a god. We are all only limited human beings and we do not know in any fundamental sense what is good and bad in a given case. We know it only abstractly. To see through a concrete situation to the bottom is God's affair alone. We may perhaps form an opinion about it but we do not know whether it is finally valid. At most we can say cautiously: judged by such and such a standard such and such a thing is good or evil, Something that appears evil to one nation [or person] may be regarded as good by another nation. This relativity of values applies also in the realm of aesthetics.[29]

Now, who can doubt the wisdom of such observations when we see them acted out daily on the world stage in the conflict between humanist and fundamentalist values, not to mention the myriad mundane antagonisms closer to home? Again, Jung was many years ahead of his time in counseling tolerance for points of view that are not naturally our own, nor can the conflict involved be underestimated.

Let the last words here be from Jung:

> The time for the "sweeping statements" so dear to the evangelizing moralist, which lighten his task in the most agreeable way, is long past. Nor can the conflict be escaped by a denial of moral values. The very idea of this is foreign to our instincts and contrary to nature. Every human group that is not actually sitting in prison will

---

[29] Ibid., par. 862.

follow its accustomed paths according to the measure of its freedom. Whatever the intellectual definition and evaluation of good and evil may be, the conflict between them can never be eradicated, for no one can ever forget it. Even the Christian who feels himself delivered from evil will, when the first rapture is over, remember the thorn in the flesh, which even St. Paul could not pluck out.[30]

This is as much as to say that the thorn in the flesh, like the fly in the ointment, may be just the curative needful.

---

[30] "The Personification of the Opposites," *Mysterium Coniunctionis,* CW 14, par. 232.

11
Psychotherapists or the Clergy

(from *Psychology and Religion: West and East,* CW 11; vintage 1932)

The reproach levelled at the Freudian and Adlerian theories is not that they are based on instincts, but that they are one-sided. It is psychology without the psyche, and this suits people who think they have no spiritual needs or aspirations. But here both doctor and patient deceive themselves. Even though the theories of Freud and Adler come much nearer to getting at the bottom of the neuroses than any earlier approach from the medical side, their exclusive concern with the instincts fails to satisfy the deeper spiritual needs of the patient. They are too much bound by the premises of nineteenth-century science, too matter of fact, and they give too little value to fictional and imaginative processes. In a word, they do not give enough meaning to life. And it is only meaning that liberates.

Ordinary reasonableness, sound human judgment, science as a compendium of common sense, these certainly help us over a good part of the road, but they never take us beyond the frontiers of life's most commonplace realities, beyond the merely average and normal. They afford no answer to the question of psychic suffering and its profound significance. A psychoneurosis must be understood, ultimately, as the suffering of a soul which has not discovered its meaning. But all creativeness in the realm of the spirit as well as every psychic advance of man arises from the suffering of the soul, and the cause of the suffering is spiritual stagnation, or psychic sterility.[31]

For many centuries it was assumed that the saving of souls was the prerogative of religion: *extra ecclesiam nulla salus* ("no salvation outside the Church").

---

[31] "Psychotherapists or the Clergy," *Psychology and Religion: West and East,* CW 11, pars. 496f.

This worked well enough as long as there were legions of believers in one or another dogmatic creed designed to provide a framework with which to understand the immediate personal experience of the unknown, and priests were accepted as mediators between heaven and earth. Nowadays, however, unbelievers far outnumber believers, so where does a suffering soul turn for surcease?

Jung was not against "religious belief"; in fact he championed it, as witness the following passage:

> Among all my patients in the second half of life—that is to say, over thirty-five—there has not been one whose problem in the last resort was not that of finding a religious outlook on life. It is safe to say that every one of them fell ill because he had lost what the living religions of every age have given to their followers, and none of them has been really healed who did not regain his religious outlook.[32]

However, Jung, himself a Swiss Protestant pastor's son who decried his father's mindless faith,[33] stressed that he was by no means referring to belief in a particular creed or membership of a church, but rather to a certain attitude of mind. He described this attitude in terms of the Latin word *religio,* from *relegere,* meaning a careful consideration and observation of irrational factors historically conceived as spirits, demons, gods, etc., "the attitude peculiar to a consciousness which has been changed by experience of the *numinosum*"—the unknown.[34]

Thus someone in a conflict situation, for instance, has to rely on

> divine comfort and mediation . . . . an autonomous psychic happening, a hush that follows the storm, a reconciling light in the darkness . . . secretly bringing order into the chaos of his soul.[35]

---

[32] Ibid., par. 509.

[33] See *Memories, Dreams, Reflections,* pp. 92ff. For comments on Jung's relationship with his father, see John P. Dourley, *A Strategy for a Loss of Faith,* pp. 13ff.

[34] "Psychology and Religion," *Psychology and Religion,* CW 11, par. 9.

[35] "A Psychological Approach to the Dogma of the Trinity," ibid., par. 260.

Jung often used the word "soul" in its traditional theological sense, but he strictly limited its psychological meaning. "By soul," he writes, "I understand a clearly demarcated functional complex that can best be described as 'personality.' "[36] Soul-making, in this secular context, can thus be seen as a natural consequence of differentiating and consciously assimilating previously unconscious contents—particularly those associated with persona, shadow, and anima or animus.

Myself, I am temperamentally prosaic. Until recently I was so taken up with what was right in front of me that I seldom thought about soul from one day to the next. But now when I do, yes, I can readily see my life in terms of soul—soulful encounters with my parts unknown. Clearly I have projected my soul onto many others (especially women), as have they onto me, and subsequently suffered its loss, as have they. Now I experience soul when I stare at the wall in the still of night. Soul is there when I am in conflict with myself, when I struggle for answers. Soul is what I am, as opposed to what I seem to be. Soul is forged in the interactions between me and my Rachel anima, and I see it daily in the material presented to me in my analytic practice.

Gordon, a forty-eight-year-old accountant, brings a dream:

A woman approaches with a child. It's a boy, a year old, maybe a bit more. The woman is vaguely familiar. She asks me for religious instruction. I tell her she's made a mistake, that I'm an atheist. She just smiles and hands me the child.

"I woke up quite mystified. What do you make of it?" he asks.
"You first," I say.
"I suppose the woman is a feminine side of myself I don't know well."
"And the child?"
"New life, new possibilities . . . ? Say, it's just over a year ago that I started seeing you. That would have been the birth of some-

---

[36] "Definitions," *Psychological Types,* CW 6, par. 797.

thing new, wouldn't it—the child?"

"And conception, nine months before that?"

"Well, let's see . . . that's when I left my wife . . ."

Maria, sixty-five-year-old artist, German by birth, survivor of an Allied concentration camp and an abusive childhood, taps the latest of the many thick journals in which for more than twenty years she has kept a faithful record of her dreams, thoughts and daily happenings.

"This is my soul," she says. "It is me."

At times of transition from one stage of life to another, traditional religious imagery often appears in dreams. A childless woman in her forties dreams of baptizing her new-born. A man in his fifties dreams of finding a long-lost baby boy under a pile of rubble—in the basement of a church. People dream of being priests or nuns, of celebrating Mass, of family seders, of pilgrimages, of mountainous journeys, fearful descents into black holes, wandering in the desert. A shopping mall becomes a cathedral. Shrines magically appear in parking lots. Virgin births and divine children— born walking and speaking—are not rare.

The particular significance of such images is inextricably bound up with the dreamer's personal history and associations, but beyond that they seem to derive from a common bedrock, the archetypal basis for all mythology and all religion—the search for meaning. Hence Jung writes, in the passage introducing this chapter—a comment worth repeating—that a neurosis "must be understood, ultimately, as the suffering of a soul which has not discovered its meaning."[37]

We can say, then, that there *is* a religious dimension to Jungian psychology, but not in the conventional sense. Analyst Marion Woodman describes it as soul-making:

> Psychological work is soul work. . . . By soul, I mean the eternal part of us that lives in this body for a few years, the timeless part of

---

[37] "Psychotherapists or the Clergy," *Psychology and Religion,* CW 11, par. 497.

ourselves that wants to create timeless objects like art, painting and architecture. Whenever the ego surrenders to the archetypal images of the unconscious, time meets the timeless. Insofar as those moments are conscious, they are psychological—they belong to the soul. . . . For me, soul-making is allowing the eternal essence to enter and experience the outer world through all the orifices of the body . . . so that the soul grows during its time on Earth. It grows like an embryo in the womb. Soul-making is constantly confronting the paradox that an eternal being is dwelling in a temporal body. That's why it suffers, and learns by heart.[38]

This is not to say that Jungian psychology is a religion. Jung himself adamantly denied anything of the sort. Yet he did believe that the human longing for consciousness is essentially a religious activity. In an essay identifying five prominent groups of instinctive drives—creativity, reflection, activity, sexuality and hunger—he included the religious urge as a subset of reflection.[39]

Marie-Louise von Franz notes that Jung came early to the recognition that institutionalized religion could give him no answers to his own psychic distress. Instead, he found the way to illumination in his own depths; thus:

The basis and substance of Jung's entire life and work do not lie in the traditions and religions which have become contents of collective consciousness, but rather in that primordial experience which is the final source of these contents: the encounter of the single individual with his own god or daimon, his struggle with the overpowering emotions, affects, fantasies and creative inspirations and obstacles which come to light from within.[40]

The religious attitude can hardly be pinned down in a sentence or two, but it certainly involves acknowledging, and paying homage to, something numinous, mysterious—something far greater than oneself. God? Nature? The Self? Take your pick.

---

[38] *Conscious Femininity: Interviews with Marion Woodman,* pp. 134f.

[39] "Psychological Factors Determining Human Behaviour," CW 8, pars. 235ff.

[40] *C.G. Jung: His Myth in Our Time,* pp. 13-14.

Analyst Lawrence Jaffe writes:

Jung says of his message that it sounds like religion, but is not. He claims to be speaking as a philosopher, whereas on other occasions he rejected even that designation, preferring to be considered an empirical scientist. Consistently he rejected the idea that he was a religious leader—an understandable reaction in view of the usual fate of founders of new religions (like Christ): dismemberment and early death.

Jung's protestations notwithstanding, his psychology can be considered a kind of religion; not a traditional religion with an emphasis on dogma, faith and ritual, to be sure, but a new kind—a religion of experience.[41]

Well, I can live with that, for when all is said and done, what is the wellspring of religion if not our experience of the gods? We sophisticated moderns may call them archetypes or complexes, but by any name they will always be essentially unknown. We may find these gods or complexes inside instead of out, but perhaps that is simply a manner of speaking. The alchemists saw little difference, according to this ancient Hermetic ditty quoted more than once by Jung:

> Heaven above
> Heaven below
> Stars above
> Stars below
> All that is above
> Also is below
> Grasp this
> And rejoice[42]

Returning now to the earlier question, where is a suffering person to turn for solace? Jung suggests as an example two ordinary, reasonable and frequent queries: What is the meaning of my life, or of life in general?—

---

[41] *Liberating the Heart: Spirituality and Jungian Psychology,* p. 19.

[42] See, for instance, "The Psychology of the Transference," *The Practice of Psychotherapy,* CW 16, par. 384.

Today people believe that they know only too well what the clergy-man will—or rather must—say to this. They smile at the very thought of the philosopher's answer, and in general do not expect much of the physician. But from the psychotherapist who analyses the unconscious—from him one might at last learn something. Per-haps he has dug up from some abstruse depths of his mind, among other things, some meaning which could even be bought for a fee! It must be a relief to every serious-minded person to hear that the psy-chotherapist also does not know what to say. Such a confession is often the beginning of the patient's confidence in him.[43]

Jung then brushes aside those persons with "negative, destruc-tive, and perverse natures—degenerates and unbalanced eccen-trics—who are never satisfied anywhere, and who therefore flock to every new banner, much to the hurt of these movements and under-takings." Jung rather favors those who

are by no means sickly eccentrics, but are very often exceptionally able, courageous, and upright persons who have repudiated tradi-tional truths for honest and decent reasons, and not from wickedness of heart. Every one of them has the feeling that our religious truths have somehow become hollow. Either they cannot reconcile the sci-entific and the religious outlook, or the Christian tenets have lost their authority and their psychological justification. People no longer feel redeemed by the death of Christ; they cannot believe—for al-though it is a lucky man who *can* believe, it is not possible to com-pel belief. Sin has become something quite relative: what is evil for one man is good for another. After all, why should not the Buddha be right too?[44]

Jung describes neurosis as "an inner cleavage—the state of being at war with oneself,"[45] and goes even further:

Healing may be called a religious problem. In the sphere of social or national relations, the state of suffering may be civil war, and this

---

[43] "Psychotherapists or the Clergy," *Psychology and Religion,* CW 11, par. 515.
[44] Ibid., par. 516.
[45] Ibid., par. 522.

state is to be cured by the Christian virtue of forgiveness and love of one's enemies. That which we recommend, with the conviction of good Christians, as applicable to external situations, we must apply inwardly in the treatment of neurosis. This is why modern man has heard enough about guilt and sin. He is sorely enough beset by his own bad conscience, and wants rather to know how to reconcile himself with his own nature—how he is to love the enemy in his own heart and call the wolf his brother.[46]

The "wolf," of course, is one's own shadow, which it is our task to accept and integrate into consciousness as much as we can, lest the split become chronic and poison every aspect of our life.

There is a mistaken collective belief that the goal of psychotherapy is to chase away the inner demons and make one a better person—wiser, more moral and a responsible citizen. But it is not like that at all. Depth analysis is aimed solely at stimulating the acquisition of self-knowledge and self-understanding, which may lead to happiness, the doing of good and greater joy, but also to greater sorrow or acts of evil.

The consequences of analysis, while not being a matter of indifference to the analyst, are out of his or her hands. Everything depends on the analysand and how she or he acts on the basis of what they have learned about themselves. The analyst does not know what is right or wrong for another person. The analyst is not unmindful of collective mores, but is more concerned with following and mapping the labyrinthine path dictated by the analysand's inner center, insofar as that can be discerned with any certitude—though the path to wholeness is always strewn with uncertain adventures and paradoxical turnings. At times it brings the light of joyful wisdom, at others it is a bed of nails, no getting around it. The analyst does not try to save people from themselves, for he or she knows not in advance what are "mistakes." The analyst is guide, mentor and facilitator, not a god-almighty authority of right and wrong. Jung expresses it like this:

> Tired of this warfare of opinions [between blind faith and reason], the modern man wishes to find out for himself how things are. And

---

[46] Ibid., par. 523.

though this desire opens the door to the most dangerous possibilities, we cannot help seeing it as a courageous enterprise and giving it some measure of sympathy. It is no reckless adventure, but an effort inspired by deep spiritual distress to bring meaning once more into life on the basis of fresh and unprejudiced experience. Caution has its place, no doubt, but we cannot refuse our support to a serious venture which challenges the whole of the personality. If we oppose it, we are trying to suppress what is best in man—his daring and aspirations. And should we succeed, we should only have stood in the way of that invaluable experience which might have given a meaning to life. What would have happened if Paul had allowed himself to be talked out of his journey to Damascus?

The psychotherapist who takes his work seriously must come to grips with this question. He must decide in every single case whether or not he is willing to stand by a human being with counsel and help upon what may be a daring misadventure. He must have no fixed ideas as to what is right and what not—otherwise he takes something from the richness of the experience.[47]

I think that is a pretty powerful statement of the strengths and limitations of analysis, and also why Jungian psychology has been called "a religion of experience."[48]

Personally, I reject the notion that Jung's ideas constitute a religion (or, as some accuse, a cult), but I am very much in favor of individual experience and all the false byways and dead ends that may entail before coming into one's personal treasure. Anyone who does not agree with this hazardous proposition may as well seek the comforting solace of a religious creed which like father and mother has ready answers and purports to heal all wounds.

It is worth repeating that Jung was not opposed to organized religion for those who find meaning in it; so he writes:

My own position is on the extreme left wing of Protestant opinion, yet I would be the first to warn people against uncritical generalizations of their own point of view. . . . Who are forgiven their many sins? Those who have loved much. But as to those who love little,

---

[47] Ibid., pars. 529f.

[48] See above, p. 38.

their few sins are held against them. I am firmly convinced that a vast number of people belong to the fold of the Catholic Church and nowhere else, because they are most suitably housed there. I am as much persuaded of this as of the fact, which I have myself observed, that a primitive religion is better suited to primitive people than Christianity, which is so incomprehensible to them and so foreign to their blood that they can only ape it in the most disgusting way. I believe, too, that there must be protestants against the Catholic Church, and also protestants against Protestantism—for the manifestations of the spirit are truly wondrous, and as varied as Creation itself.[49]

Finally, in the essay immediately following this one in the *Collected Works,* Jung makes clear the distance between depth psychology and pastoral care:

The cure of souls as practised by the clergyman or priest is a religious influence based on a Christian confession of faith. Psychoanalysis, on the other hand, is a medical intervention, a psychological technique whose purpose it is to lay bare the contents of the unconscious and integrate them into the conscious mind.[50]

—though nevertheless he is hopeful and conciliatory:

It is easier for the Catholic clergy to employ the elements of psychological analysis than it is for the Protestant. The latter are faced with the harder task. Not only do the Catholics possess a ready-made pastoral technique in the historically sanctioned form of confession, penance, and absolution, but they also have at their command a rich and palpably ritualistic symbolism which fully satisfies the demands as well as the obscure passions of simpler minds. . . . The doctor and the clergyman undoubtedly clash head-on in analytical psychology. This collision should lead to co-operation and not to enmity.[51]

---

[49] Ibid., par. 537.

[50] "Psychoanalysis and the Cure of Souls," *Psychology and Religion,* CW 11, par. 539.

[51] Ibid., par. 548. See below, chap. 18, "The Symbolic Life," for more extensive comments by Jung on the efficacy of Catholic rituals.

Myself, I find solace in the work of Jung, the arms of MP (my paramour), romantic ballads and Rilke's *Duino Elegies*:

> Who, if I cried, would hear me from the order
> of Angels? And even if one suddenly held me
> to his heart: I would dissolve there from
> his stronger presence. For beauty is only
> the beginning of a terror we can just barely endure,
> and what we so admire is its calm
> disdaining to destroy us. Every Angel brings terror.
> So I withhold myself and keep back the lure
> of my dark sobbing.[52]

And here endeth this lesson, except for a personal addendum:

I recently asked MP if I had seduced her, or vice versa.

She smiled: "You may remember the Russian fairy tale, "The Virgin Czar," where the Baba Yaga witch asks the hero as he passes by her hut on chicken-bone stilts, 'Are you going on this journey voluntarily or involuntarily?' "

"Yes," I laughed, "I do now. According to von Franz it's a trick of the mother complex. One could spend hours tying oneself up in knots trying to answer such a philosophical question when action is required. The hero's proper response is, 'Shut up and make my dinner!'"[53]

"So get on with you," said MP, "and I'll prepare a collation!"

No wonder I have some difficulty distinguishing between MP and Rachel. I m besotted with them both, but it's no contest really, because MP is flesh and blood, and so she is bound to have the upper hand, sometimes to Rachel's chagrin.

---

[52] "The First Elegy," in Rainer Maria Rilke, *The Duino Elegies,* p. 35.
[53] See Mare-Louise -von Franz, in *Puer Atrnus,* pp 173ff.

12

The Psychic Nature of the Alchemical Work

(from *Psychology and Alchemy,* CW 12; vintage 1937)

[The eighteenth century] was a time when the mind of the alchemist was still grappling with the problems of matter, when the exploring consciousness was confronted by the dark void of the unknown, in which figures and laws were dimly perceived and attributed to matter although they really belonged to the psyche. Everything unknown and empty is filled with psychological projection; it is as if the investigator's own psychic background were mirrored in the darkness. What he sees in matter, or thinks he can see, is chiefly the data of his own unconscious which he is projecting into it. In other words, he encounters in matter, as apparently belonging to it, certain qualities and potential meanings of whose psychic nature he is entirely unconscious. This is particularly true of classical alchemy, when empirical science and mystical philosophy were more or less undifferentiated.[54]

The alchemical *opus* deals in the main not just with chemical experiments as such, but with something resembling psychic processes expressed in pseudochemical language. The ancients knew more or less what chemical processes were; therefore they must have known that the thing they practised was, to say the least of it, no ordinary chemistry.[55]

What was alchemy? Apparently it is still of contemporary interest, for when I Googled "alchemy" I garnered 16,600,000 hits. . . .

Well, it was surely the origin, the precursor, of modern chemistry. But was it, as popularly believed, simply a misguided attempt to change lead into gold? Were the alchemists just greedy-guts interested in monetary gain? And what does it have to do with us?

---

[54] "Basic Concepts of Alchemy," *Psychology and Alchemy,* CW 12, par. 332
[55] "The Psychic Nature of the Alchemical Work," ibid., par. 342.

Figure 2. The double face of alchemy—laboratory and library—corresponds to the twofold nature of the individuation process: the active participation in outer reality and relationships, together with the process of inner reflection.

First things first. Alchemical practices flourished widely in Greek and Roman territories over many years from the first century A.D. But to modern logical minds the practice of alchemy seems whimsical and foolhardy. It is in fact virtually impenetrable unless the symbolism involved is understood—and this is the immense task Jung undertook to accomplish in his later years.

It was the genius of Jung to discern in the field of alchemy and Hermetic philosophy a parallel to the psychological individuation process. His several books on the subject show that although the "pseudochemistry" of alchemy and the process of individuation do not at first glance have much in common, at bottom they are both concerned with the search for emotional balance and well-being, through the discrimination and synthesis of opposites. In other words, it was not the *aurium vulgi* (filthy lucre) that the alchemists sought in the *prima materia* (base material, lead), but the philosophical gold, the so-called *lapis philosophorum* or Philosophers' Stone. Indeed, the secret art of alchemy lay in the transformation of the personality; what the alchemists thought of as releasing the spirit imprisoned in matter is metaphorically analogous to the conscious assimilation of unconscious contents.

Alchemical texts are notoriously cryptic, virtually a secret language. In trying to understand them, one risks falling into what the practitioners themselves called "the madness of the lead."[56] In layman's language, this would be a psychosis, a sudden eruption of unconscious contents into consciousness.

Jung wrote numerous essays and three massive books on the symbolic and psychological significance of alchemy: *Psychology and Alchemy,* CW 12; *Aion: Researches into the Phenomenology of the Self* (CW 9ii); and *Mysterium Coniunctionis: An Inquiry into the Separation and Synthesis of Psychic Opposite in Alchemy* (CW 14).The last two mentioned are particularly dense and not easy to follow without the insightful companion volumes authored by Edward F. Edinger and Marie-Louise von Franz.[57]

Jung was the first to discover the symbolic and psychological significance of alchemy. Well, perhaps "discover" is too strong a word, for its allegorical nature was already apprehended; rather he became aware that alchemical practices were analogous to the circuitous process of individuation he witnessed in his psychiatric practice, a process that eventually became the cornerstone of his school of analytical psychology. He recognized that the *lapis* or

---

[56] Also known as *afflictio animae,* or sickness of the soul, which threatens anyone who strives to understand the ineffable.

[57] See Edinger, *The Aion Lectures* and *The Mysterium Lectures: A Journey Through Jung's* Mysterium Coniunctionis; *The Mystery of the Coniunctio: Alchemical Image of Individuation,* and *Anatomy of the Psyche: Alchemical Symbolism in Psychotherapy.* See also von Franz, *Alchemy: An Introduction* and *Aurora Consurgens: On the Problem of Opposites in Alchemy.*

Philosophers' Stone the alchemists sought was not actually *aurum vulgaris* but a much more substantial treasure—their own wholeness. And this happened, or did not, through the natural phenomenon of projection:

> The real nature of matter was unknown to the alchemist: he knew it only in hints. In seeking to explore it he projected the unconscious into the darkness of matter in order to illuminate it. In order to explain the mystery of matter he projected yet another mystery—his own unknown psychic background—into what was to be explained: *Obscurium per obscurius, ignotum per ignotius!* [the obscure through the obscure, ignorance through ignorance]. This procedure was not, of course, intentional; it was an involuntary occurrence.[58]

Jung goes on here to reminds us that projection is not made, not a conscious act; it happens, it is simply there:

> In the darkness of anything external to me I find, without recognizing it as such, an interior or psychic life that is my own. . . .I am therefore inclined to assume that the real root of alchemy is to be sought less in philosophical doctrines than in the projections of individual investigators. I mean by this that while working on his chemical experiments the operator had certain psychic experiences which appeared to him as the particular behaviour of the chemical process. Since it was a question of projection, he was naturally unconscious of the fact that the experience had nothing to do with matter itself (that is, with matter as we know it today). He experienced his projection as a property of matter, but what he was in reality experiencing was his own unconscious. In this way he recapitulated the whole history of man's knowledge of nature.[59]

As we know, science began with the study of the stars, and mankind discovered in them the dominants of the unconscious, the "gods," as well as the curious psychological qualities of the zodiac—a complete projected theory of human character. Astrology is

---

[58] Ibid., par. 315.

[59] Ibid., par. 346.

in fact a primordial experience similar to alchemy. Such projections repeat themselves whenever we try to explore an empty darkness and involuntarily fill it with ourselves—just as we regularly fall in love with a pretty face without knowing who or what is behind it.

So what can we learn about ourselves from alchemy? Why should we make the effort? Why spend precious time away from loved ones, sporting events, ballrooms, opera or museums to try to understand the medieval mind? Good and valid questions, to which there is only one answer, Jung's: "Without consciousness things go less well."[60] As it happens, with consciousness things go less easily too, but that's another story, for another book.

In any case, even some very serious students of analytical psychology shy away from coming to grips with the psychological significance of alchemy. They thereby escape the madness of the lead, but also miss widening their consciousness.

Consider the following comparison of the stages of enlightenment, according to the alchemical *opus,* and what happens as we become progressively more conscious:

Alchemy	Individuation
nigredo (blackening)	confrontation with shadow
albedo (whitening)	integration of complexes
rubedo (reddening)	relationship with the Self

Marie-Louise von Franz explains these stages as follows:

The *nigredo* has its parallels . . . in the confrontation with the shadow. Everything which one has criticized, with moral indignation, in others, is "served up" in dreams as a part of one's own being. Envy, jealousy, lies, sexual drives, desire for power, ambition, greed for money, irritability, all kinds of childishness suddenly stare implacably at one, out of one's dreams. Illusions about oneself and the world fall apart, ideals are revealed as desire for power in disguise, "sacred" convictions as hollow.[61]

---

[60] "Psychology and '*Weltanschauung,*' " *The Structue and Dynamics of the Psyche,* CW 8, par. 695.

[61] *C.G. Jung: His Myth in Our Time,* pp. 222f.

In the alchemical work the *nigredo* is followed by the *albedo*. This phase corresponds in the individuation process to the integration of the inner contrasexual components, the anima in the case of a man, the animus with a woman. . . . Psychologically it is a question of the transference problem, the constellation of a love relation between doctor and patient, or else the problem of a great and passionate love which is just as often constellated outside the therapeutic situation.[62]

In the alchemical procedure the *rubedo* . . . follows the *albedo*. In this phase the work comes to an end, the retort is opened and the philosophers' stone begins to radiate a cosmically healing effect. . . . The Self, too, which is brought into reality in the individuation process, is the wider, inner man who reaches toward eternity, the Anthropos who is described [in alchemical works] as spherical and bisexual and who "stands for the mutual integration of conscious and unconscious."[63]

"That is very heady stuff," said my Rachel muse, suddenly by my side, and welcome.

"Yes, but don't fret," I said, hugging her, "I will walk you through it."

So, here's what arcane alchemical procedures might look like in a person's life:

First, the *nigredo*—all those things about ourselves that we don't like or feel embarrassed about, like smoking dope, watching porn movies or lusting after our neighbor's wife. And then there's our unexplored potential, our unlived life. All that is part of our shadow.

Then the *albedo,* which involves acknowledging that we have a contrasexual side, an inner man/woman with whom we must establish a relationship for the sake of our psychic health.

Next, the *rubedo* involves dealing with the opposites— differentiating good from bad, want from need, personal values from those dictated by the collective. Constellated opposites activate in turn the

---

[62] Ibid., p. 223.
[63] Ibid., p. 227.

archetype of the crucifixion, which is ubiquitous in the Western unconscious, whether we adhere to Christian beliefs or not. In short, we are torn between this and that, in conflict with ourselves.

Differentiating opposites always entails suffering. There is no way around it, and those who are not up to it had better not go into analysis, for the analytic process focuses long-term on the integration of opposites. The more conscious you become, the more you are obliged to suffer the tension between opposites.

All the above is succinctly summed up in the ancient alchemical saying known as the Axiom of Maria. It goes like this: "One becomes two, two becomes three, and out of the third comes the one as the fourth."[64] Jung saw this dictum as an apt metaphor for the process of individuation, a progressive advance of consciousness in which conflict plays a profoundly important part.

In brief, *one* stands for the original, paradisiacal state of unconscious wholeness (e.g., childhood); *two* signifies the conflict between opposites (e.g., persona and shadow); *three* points to a potential resolution; *the third* is the transcendent function[65]; and *the one as the fourth* is code for the Philosophers' Stone—psychologically equivalent to a transformed state of conscious wholeness.

Consciously pursuing individuation also usually involves sacrifice. Jung has written a good deal on the subject, particularly as it relates to the Christian myth in general and the Catholic Church's ritual of the Mass in particular.[66]

However, outside the context of organized religion, Jung believed that the basic psychological issue in sacrifice was to give up one's attachment to infantile values and satisfactions:

> Sacrifice means giving up the connection with the mother, relinquishing all the ties and limitations which the psyche has taken over

---

[64] "Introduction to the Religious and Psychological Problems of Alchemy," *Psychology and Alchemy,* CW 12, par. 26

[65] See *Jung Uncorked,* Book One, chap. 8.

[66] See "Transformation Symbolism in the Mass," *Psychology and Religion,* CW 11.

from childhood into adult life. . . . It is not possible to live too long amid infantile surroundings, or in the bosom of the family, without endangering one's psychic health. Life calls us forth to independence, and anyone who does not heed this call because of childish laziness or timidity is threatened with neurosis. . . .

. . . The whole of the libido is needed for the battle of life.[67]

Indeed, the main strength of Jung's writings on alchemy was not the demystification of the "holy technique" of the practice. No, it is rather that he brought to light the fact that the images and motifs that so occupied the alchemists are of an archetypal nature, and as such constantly crop up in the dreams, drawings and fantasies of modern individuals.

It follows, then, that anyone involved with his or her psychological development is in effect an alchemist, and Jung's work is first and foremost a practical guide to what is going on in the laboratory of the unconscious. Edinger concurs:

The great value of alchemical images is that they give us an *objective* basis from which to approach dreams and other unconscious material. With the psyche more than with any other subject it is very difficult to distinguish between objective fact and personal bias. A working knowledge of alchemical images can be very helpful in promoting this much needed objectivity.[68]

---

[67] *Symbols of Transformation,* CW 5, pars. 461ff.

[68] *Anatomy of the Psyche,* preface, p. xix.

13
The Spirit Mercurius
(from *Alchemical Studies,* CW 13;
vintage 1942/1953)

In my contribution to [this symposium] I will try to show that this many-hued and wily god did not by any means die with the decline of the classical era, but on the contrary has gone on living in strange guises through the centuries, even into recent times, and has kept the mind of man busy with his deceptive arts and healing gifts.[69]

One simple and unmistakable term in no way sufficed to designate what the alchemists had in mind when they spoke of Mercurius. It was certainly quicksilver, but a very special quicksilver, "our" Mercurius, the essence, moisture, or principle behind or within the quicksilver—that indefinable, fascinating, irritating, and elusive thing which attracts an unconscious projection.[70]

Mercurius, as the above passages imply, is one of the most elusive figures or concepts in the whole alchemical canon, for he is at once a chemical substance and a spiritual essence that pervades all aspects of the *opus.*

Jung begins his discussion with a detailed analysis of the Grimm fairy tale, "The Spirit in the Bottle," a medieval story so widely known in other versions and traditions that it qualifies as an archetypal motif. The essentials are briefly stated as follows:

A poor woodcutter's son roaming the forest comes upon a massive old oak. He hears a voice calling from the ground: "Let me out, let me out!" The boy digs down and discovers a sealed glass bottle from which apparently the voice has come. He opens it and instantly a spirit rushes out and soon becomes as big as the oak. Now this spirit howls that he will have his revenge for being confined in the

---

[69] "The Spirit Mercurius," *Alchemical Studies,* CW 13, par. 239.

[70] Ibid., par. 259.

Figure 3. The transformation of Mercurius, as *prima materia,* in the heated, sealed vessel is comparable to cooking the basic instinctive drives in their own affect until their essential fantasy content becomes conscious. "Instead of arguing with the drives which carry us away, we prefer to cook them and . . . ask them what they want. . . . That can be discovered by active imagination, or through a fantasy, or through experimenting in reality, but always with the introverted attitude of observing objectively what the drive really wants."[71]

---

[71] Von Franz, *Alchemy,* p. 129.

bottle, and he threatens to strangle the lad. The boy, being quick witted, conceives of a trick. "First," he says, "you must prove to me that you are the same spirit that was shut up in that little bottle." The spirit agrees and shrinks meekly back into the flask. The boy immediately seals it and the spirit is caught again.

Now the spirit promises to reward the boy richly if he will let him out. The lad does so and is rewarded with a small piece of rag. The spirit says, "If you spread one end of this over a wound it will heal, and if you rub steel or iron with the other end it will turn into silver." The boy rubs his damaged axe with the rag and the axe turns to silver which he subsequently sells for a small fortune that enables him to go on with his studies. The rag works on wounds too and the boy later becomes a rich and famous doctor.[72]

Jung treats this tale as he would a dream or a fantasy—as a spontaneous statement of the unconscious about itself. He thereupon proposes a rather ingenious interpretation of its various elements, an elucidation which may strike some readers as whimsical, while those familiar with the intuitive, right-brain method of amplification will surely applaud:

The fairytale mentions the forest as the place of the magic happening. The forest, dark and impenetrable to the eye, like deep water and the sea, is the container of the unknown and the mysterious. It is an appropriate synonym for the unconscious. . . . Trees, like fishes in the water, represent the living contents of the unconscious. Among these contents one of special significance is characterized as an "oak." Trees have individuality. A tree, therefore, is often a symbol of personality. . . . The mighty old oak is proverbially the king of the forest. Hence it represents a central figure among the contents of the unconscious, possessing personality in the most marked degree. It is the prototype of the *self,* a symbol of the source and goal of the individuation process. The oak stands for the still unconscious core of the personality, the plant symbolism indicating a state of deep unconsciousness. From this it may be concluded that the hero of the

---

[72] Ibid., par. 239, condensed; paraphrased from Grimm Brothers, *The Complete Grimm's Fairy Tales,* pp. 458ff.

fairytale is profoundly unconscious of himself . . . . not yet "enlightened." For our hero, therefore, the tree conceals a great secret.

The secret is hidden not in the top but in the roots of the tree; and since it is, or has, a personality it also possesses the most striking marks of personality—voice, speech, and conscious purpose, and it demands to be set free by the hero. . . . The roots extend into the inorganic realm, into the mineral kingdom. In psychological terms, this would mean that the self has its roots in the body, indeed in the body's chemical elements. . . . The alchemists described their four elements as *radices,* corresponding to the Empedoclean *rhizomata,* and in them they saw the constituents of the most significant and central symbol of alchemy, the *lapis philsophorum,* which represents the goal of the individuation process.[73]

Wait, there's more:

The secret hidden in the roots is a spirit sealed inside a bottle. Naturally it was not hidden away among the roots to start with, but was first confined in a bottle, which was then hidden. Presumably a magician, that is an alchemist, caught and imprisoned it. As we shall see later, this spirit is something like the numen of the tree, its *spiritus vegetativus,* which is one of the definitions of Mercurius. As the life principle of the tree . . . it could also be described as the *principium individuationis* [principle of individuation].[74]

Jung sums up the foregoing as follows:

So if we translate it into psychological language, the fairytale tells us that the mercurial essence, the *principium individuationis,* would have developed freely under natural conditions but was robbed of its freedom by deliberate intervention from outside, and was artfully confined and banished like an evil spirit.[75]

And if that was so, asks Jung, who deemed the spirit to be evil and confined and banished it? Why, the Catholic Church of course,

---

[73] Ibid., pars. 241f.

[74] Ibid., par. 243.

[75] Ibid., par. 244.

and Christianity in general with its doctrine of original sin and contempt for the body as the root of all evil. Jung's thesis is therefore that the magician/alchemist, in cahoots with his *soror mystica* (female assistant), hid the genie/spirit to protect it from the inhospitable cultural environment and provide an earthy spirit compensatory to the Church's designation of Christ as Logos.

Mercurius is the fly in the ointment, the invisible little guy who ruins your plans. He is mercurial, after all, unpredictable; there's no telling when he might pop up in your life to turn it topsy-turvy, from driving you into a lamp-post to having a go at the baby sitter. And you can be conscious of his trickster quality and still be at his mercy. Mercurius is second cousin to the aliens who abduct you from hot tubs and break ankles.[76]

Of course, like any archetypal entity Mercurius embodies the opposites, and so he has a benign side as well. He gets you out of bed in the morning; he gives you ambition, ideas "out of the blue," a job to do, someone to love, kids to focus on with awe.

Given the alchemical association of Mercurius with the body, it is no surprise that the Church had a role in burying him. "The Spirit in the Bottle" is a cautionary tale compensating the Church's long-standing fear of untrammeled instinct and aversion to the flesh. The fairy tale compensates this stance by redeeming the sleeping spirit, *materia,* but note, not without some effort on the part of the wily Dummling who is richly rewarded for his insight, as are we all, not with gold—though sometimes that as well—but with *joie de vivre* if we attend to our psychological health.

Much more could be said about Mercurius, but perhaps it is enough to end this with Jung's comprehensive summary:

1. Mercurius consists of all conceivable opposites. He is thus quite obviously a duality but is named a unity in spite of the fact that his innumerable inner contradictions can dramatically fly apart into an equal number of disparate and apparently independent figures.

---

[76] See *Jung Uncorked,* Book One, p. 80.

2. He is both material and spiritual.

3. He is the process by which the lower and material is transformed into the higher and spiritual, and vice versa.

4. He is the devil, a redeeming psychopomp, an evasive trickster, and God's reflection in physical nature.

5. He is also the reflection of a mystical experience of the artifex [practitioner] that coincides with the *opus alchymicum.*

6. As such, he represents on the one hand the self and on the other the individuation process and, because of the limitless number of his names, also the collective unconscious.[77]

Truly, as von Franz observes,

It is one of Jung's greatest achievements, the significance of which has not yet been adequately recognized, that he rediscovered the projected religious myth of alchemy and showed unmistakably *where* it originated and where it is still at work today, not in matter but in the *objective unconscious psyche* of Western man.[78]

There is news currently of a "good-bye to God" movement building up in America—millions banding together and declaring themselves atheists—a foreseeable compensation for the one-sided militancy of fundamentalist believers.

Alas, they all miss the point, for the real issue is not the existence or not of God but the ineffable Mystery—the *mysterium tremendum.* The god of Reason rises up to smight the irrational! And behind both is Mercurius. When will we realize that we are not free agents? That too is the mystery plumbed by depth psychology.

---

[77] Ibid., par. 284.

[78] *C.G. Jung: His Myth in Our Time,* p. 201.

14

The Personification of the Opposites

(from *Mysterium Coniunctionis,* CW 14;
vintage 1955-56)

*Note: This chapter contains material not suitable for children of
any age. Reader discretion is advised.*

Our reason is often influenced far too much by purely physical con-
siderations, so that the union of the sexes seems to it the only sensible thing and the urge for union the most sensible instinct of all. But
if we conceive of nature in the higher sense as the totality of all phenomena, then the physical is only one of her aspects, the other is
pneumatic or spiritual. The first has always been regarded as feminine, the second as masculine. The goal of the one is union, the goal
of the other is discrimination. Because it overvalues the physical,
our contemporary reason lacks spiritual orientation, that is,
pneuma.[79]

Consciousness requires as its necessary counterpart a dark, latent,
non-manifest side, the unconscious, whose presence can be known
only by the light of consciousness. Just as the day-star rises out of
the nocturnal sea, so, ontogenetically and phylogenetically, consciousness is born of unconsciousness and sinks back every night to
this primal condition. This duality of our psychic life is the prototype and archetype of the Sol-Luna symbolism. So much did the alchemist sense the duality of his unconscious assumptions that, in the
face of all astronomical evidence, he equipped the sun with a
shadow [*sol niger*].[80]

This is one of my favorite sections in the entire *Collected Works.*
As the centerpiece of *Mysterium,* Jung's most substantial work on
alchemy, it runs for many pages and its erudition is both baffling
and challenging. Like a well-mannered Fourth of July garden party

---

[79] "The Personification of the Opposites," *Mysterium Coniunctionis,* CW 14, par.
104.

[80] Ibid., par. 117.

it builds up to a dazzling fireworks display—a lengthy and quite unexpected consideration of the symbolism and psychological interpretation of the *aqua permanens* or *sal sapientiae,* ordinary salt, of all things. The denouement makes the struggle more than worthwhile and the party conversation seem completely vapid. Indeed, plunge anywhere into CW 14 and you risk being assailed by the madness of the lead.

In alchemical writings the opposites always begin with reflections on the nature of king and queen, *sol*/sun and *luna*/moon, or in plain language the bonds and bounds of male and female, which reach their ultimate consummation in the "chymical wedding," the enigmatic *coniunctio* (conjunction) in which natural opposites are eventually united in a harmonious whole known to the alchemists as the *unus mundus* (one world). But that's only if the *sol niger* (black sun, or shadow of consciousness) doesn't interfere with the nuptials.

In both alchemical lore and Jung's understanding of psychic reality, *sol* and *luna* equate with masculine consciousness (Logos) and feminine consciousness (Eros), respectively, as follows:

> By Logos I meant discrimination, judgment, insight, and by Eros I meant the capacity to relate. I regarded both concepts as intuitive ideas which cannot be defined accurately or exhaustively. From the scientific point of view this is regrettable, but from a practical one it has its value, since the two concepts mark out a field of experience which it is equally difficult to define.[81]

Now, remember, these are archetypal qualities, biologically latent but not necessarily applicable to any particular man or woman. Opposites are everywhere, and so is paradox. See how cleverly Jung acknowledges this in order to get out of the corner he has knowingly painted himself into:

> As we can hardly ever make a psychological proposition without immediately having to reverse it, instances to the contrary leap to

---

[81] "The Personification of the Opposites," *Mysterium Coniunctionis,* CW 14, par. 224.

the eye at once: men who care nothing for discrimination, judgment or insight, and women who display an almost excessively masculine proficiency in this respect. I would like to describe such cases as the regular exceptions. They demonstrate, to my mind, the common occurrence of a psychically predominant contrasexuality. Wherever this exists we find a forcible intrusion of the unconscious, a corresponding exclusion of the consciousness specific to either sex, predominance of the shadow and of contrasexuality, and to a certain extent even the presence of symptoms of possession . . . This inversion of roles is probably the chief psychological source for the alchemical concept of the hermaphrodite. In a man it is the lunar anima, in a woman the solar animus, that influences consciousness in the highest degree.[82]

In other words, Jung suggests that a reversal of type, so to speak, is due to the influence of one's contrasexual side, the anima or animus. Like any complex, they are always more or less unconscious and active behind the scenes, though sometimes, Jung implies, they may be front and center and dominate the personality. In a man, psychologically speaking, we would call this anima-possession, in a woman animus-possession. In alchemical terms, where Logos (the masculine principle) and Eros (feminine principle) are intuitive equivalents of the archetypal images of Sol and Luna, either would manifest as the *sol niger,* or dark sun, which contaminates the otherwise "pure" light of consciousness and incidentally may explain why the alchemists so often fell short of actually producing gold.

Then follows Jung's extraordinary exploration of the meaning of salt. After many references to obscure alchemical texts on salt as "the arcane substance" associated with the parting of the Red Sea, the *anima mundi* (world soul) and "the fruitful white earth," he festoons the mind with these bold remarks:

Apart from its lunar wetness and its terrestrial nature, the most outstanding properties of salt are bitterness and wisdom. As in the double quaternio of the elements and qualities, earth and water have

---

[82] Ibid., par. 225.

coldness in common, so bitterness and wisdom would form a pair of opposites with a third thing between [see below, Figure 4]. The factor common to both, however incommensurable the two ideas may seem, is, psychologically, the function of *feeling*. Tears, sorrow, and disappointment are bitter, but wisdom is the comforter in all psychic suffering. Indeed, bitterness and wisdom form a pair of alternatives: where there is bitterness wisdom is lacking, and where wisdom is there can be no bitterness. Salt, as the carrier of this fateful alternative, is co-ordinated with the nature of woman [i.e., Eros].[83]

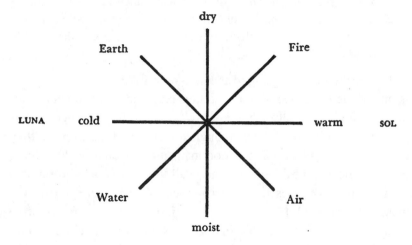

Figure 4. Double quaternio of elements and qualities.

Jung ends his deliberations on salt by skewering men:

Despite all attempts at denial and obfuscation there is an unconscious factor, a black sun, which is responsible for the surprisingly common phenomenon of masculine split-mindedness, when the right hand mustn't know what the left is doing. This split in the masculine psyche and the regular darkening of the moon in woman together explain the remarkable fact that the woman is accused of all the darkness in a man, while he himself basks in the thought that he is a veritable fount of vitality and illumination for all the females in

---

[83] Ibid., par. 530.

his environment. Actually, he would be better advised to shroud the brilliance of his mind in the profoundest doubt.[84]

So much for directed thinking. Now lend an ear to *sol niger*.

Readers will recall my client George's obsession with the now legendary Ms. Cotton Pants, recounted above in chapter 9.

Well, as it happens, I had some dealings with this winsome lovely a few years after George stopped seeing me. She turned up one afternoon in the back row of a university lecture hall in which I was teaching a class in Alchemy 101. There was no mistaking Ms. Cotton Pants—still cute, identifiably a thirty-something excheer-leader, underdressed in skimpy tank top and tight tartan mini-skirt. She could hardly sit still and seemed intensely interested in my dis-course, occasionally voicing her appreciation. She smiled at me and waved when the class was over.

Now, there's no denying that such a woman was tailor-made to engage my attention at that time in my life. I was thirty-eight years old, half-bald, divorced, lonely, penniless and going nowhere in the academic world. I was crazy about Jung and had fantasies of going to Zurich to train as an analyst. Nevertheless, I forgot about Ms. Cotton Pants until a few days later when she came to my office.

She knocked and sidled in wearing the same provocative outfit

"Dr. Razor," she said, "am I disturbing you?"

"Not at all," I replied rather grumpily, for I was cozily engaged in self-pity. "Please, have a seat."

Ms. Cotton Pants considered the options and chose a straight-back wing-chair. She sat and unlocked her knees, revealing what might be called her alter ego, Ms. Cotton Pant-less.

My mood changed. My *puer* woke up. Mercurius stirred. Projec-tions were flying. I was acutely in need of a *soror mystica* to save me from the madness of the lead. Someone more physically acces-sible than the elusive, ethereal Rachel. I moved to the couch and patted a cushion. "You'll be more comfortable here," I smiled.

---

[84] Ibid., par. 352.

In a trice she was beside me with her head tucked under my chin. Her hands roved up and down my body. I fondled her elfin ears. "I just love psychology!" she cooed, "but what does it all mean, and is alchemy practical?"

I affected a worldly manner. "Well, I could tell you astonishing tales of the *tertium non datur,* the *sine qua non* and the medieval Axiom of Maria, but that would be getting ahead of ourselves, so first," I said, guiding one of her hands lower, "the *prima materia.*"

Ms. Cotton Pants tentatively explored the bulging front of my trousers. "It's alive!" she cried.

"You betcher cotton panties," I agreed, "and he speaks!"

Then we heard a voice: "Let me out! Let me out!"

Ms. Cotton Pants beat me to the zipper, and out popped Mercurius in a gnarled sealed vessel as long as an arm.

"Holy petunia!" whooped Ms. Cotton Pants, "it's a retort!"

"Cooped up in the *vas* these many months," I observed.

"I have had my punishment and I will be avenged!" cried Mr. M.

The wily Ms. Cotton Pants considered. "Fair enough," she said, "but first prove that you big fella were actually in that small space."

Mr. M. shriveled back in. Ms. Cotton Pants zipped me up and he was caught again. Now Mr. M. promised to reward her richly if she let him out. "Release me and I will repay you with precious gems and the secret of the *filius philosophorum!*"

Ms. Cotton Pants unzipped me again and whipped her tight skirt off with a whistle. Mr. M. rushed out with gusto and nudged her pretty pudendum. "Let me in, let me in!" he cried.

Ms. Cotton Pants gasped as she angled herself to receive the twisted root. After a few minutes she got up, slipped her undergear back on and left without a word. Mr. M. retreated to his lair.

I never saw Ms. Cotton Pants again, in or out of class, but recently I read that in her guise as the esteemed Dr. Vivian Flatbush, director of the Burgholzli Clinic in Zurich, she was awarded the Nobel prize in medicine for discovering a cure for schizophrenia.

I sent her flowers, the least I could do.

15
Psychology and Literature
(from *The Spirit in Man, Art, and Literature,* CW 15;
vintage 1930/1950)

There is a fundamental difference of attitude between the psychologist's approach to a literary work and that of a literary critic. What is of decisive importance and value for the latter may be quite irrelevant for the former. Indeed, literary products of highly dubious merit are often of the greatest interest to the psychologist. The so-called "psychological novel" is by no means as rewarding for the psychologist as the literary-minded suppose. Considered as a self-contained whole, such a novel explains itself. It has done its own work of psychological interpretation, and the psychologist can at most criticize or enlarge upon this.[85]

Nobody knows what goes on when you write a book. There are theories and opinions, but nobody really *knows*. The only sure thing is that there are as many different ways to write as there are writers.

Some say they till the ground, plant the seed and watch it grow. For me it's like assembling a patchwork quilt. My computer is little more than a sewing machine. I have the patches; it's the needles that give me a hard time. Which reminds me of the poet Rilke's fictional mother's lament:

> To others she simply said by way of excuse, "I really cannot digest anything any more; but don't let that trouble you; I feel very well indeed." But to me she would suddenly turn . . . and say with a smile that cost her a severe effort, "What a lot of needles there are, Malte, and how they lie about everywhere, and when you think how easily they might fall out. . . ." She tried to say this playfully, but terror shook her at the thought of all the insecurely fastened needles which might at any instant, anywhere, fall into something.[86]

---

[85] "Psychology and Literature," *The Spirit in Man, Art, and Literature,* CW 15, par. 136.

[86] Rainer Maria Rilke, *The Notebook of Malte Laurids Brigge.*, p. 80.

Indeed, needles, sharp and pointed, as a symbol of discrimination, would wreak havoc on our culture if they were to get loose.

Jung had something to say on the subject of writing. Of course he didn't *know* either, but he had some ideas. In this volume of the *Collected Works* there are several essays that deal particularly with the creative way. One is on James Joyce and one is on Picasso; the others are more general.

Here is Jung's basic standpoint:

> The practice of art is a psychological activity and, as such, can be approached from a psychological angle. Considered in this light, art, like any other human activity deriving from psychic motives, is a proper subject for psychology. This statement, however, involves a very definite limitation of the psychological viewpoint when we come to apply it in practice. Only that aspect of art which consists in the process of artistic creation can be a subject for psychological study, but not that which constitutes its essential nature. The question of what art is in itself can never be answered by the psychologist, but must be approached from the side of aesthetics.[87]

"Huh!" said Rachel. "Already he's hedging."

Ah, she's been hiding in the weeds or stayed too long at the fair, I bet. But she is a free agent, I don't begrudge her days off, so long as she shows up when needed.

"No, he's not," I said. "He's laying down ground rules. He's setting limits to what psychology can meaningfully say about art."

"Sure," nodded Rachel, "that's his way. He'll go on like that for a hundred pages and at the end, in the very last paragraph, he'll admit he knows nothing at all."

I was surprised at Rachel's scorn.

"Look," I said, "the way I understand it, Jung is simply saying that the process of creating is a legitimate subject for psychological speculation. But psychology can't determine whether the end result is art or not. That depends on contemporary taste. Van Gogh, for

---

[87] "On the Relation of Analytical Psychology to Poetry," *The Spirit in Man, Art, and Literature,* CW 17, par. 97.

instance, died poor. Today his work fetches millions. Kafka was not appreciated in his lifetime. Now his work is hailed as a milestone in the history of modern literature."

"So?" said Rachel. "It all comes down to we know what we like."

"Oh? Why do we like what we like?"

"Well," said Rachel, "because it's art."

This would go nowhere.

"Okay," I agreed. "Never mind all the factors involved in what we like, the things we call art. But how did what we like, or not, come to be? Think about that. Why did Michelangelo sweat his guts out painting the Sistine Chapel on his back? Where did Leonardo da Vinci get the idea for flying machines four hundred years before they existed? What inspired Jackson Pollock to throw paint at canvas when nobody else did? What possessed Picasso?"

Rachel took that in. I gave her another example, closer to home.

"Where did the idea to write about Norman come from?[88] Don't ask if he's real or not, or if it's art. How did I come to put energy into his story? Or this book? I'd rather play snooker any day, or stare at the wall. But here I am, glued to the computer. Who or what is responsible? What stirs me up?"

Rachel knit her brow. A wisp of hair fluttered on her cheek. She brushed it back. A sexy woman in the prime of life. I love her. She is unpredictable, mercurial, but generally supportive.

"God?" she offered.

Good grief! What does she have between her ears? God used to be an okay explanation for everything, but not in this day and age.

I shook my head. "I hardly think so."

And lucky too. If I did, I might be out there with the rest of them, touting the Word. I'd have a program on prime-time teevee, turning lead into gold. I'd have a theme park dedicated to my mother. People who couldn't afford to would send me money. I'd put it in the

---

[88] See my *Survival Papers: Anatomy of a Midlife Crisis,* and *Dear Gladys: The Survival Papers, Book Two.*

bank and feel righteous. I'd be bigger than my boots, a goner.

"God, if he exists," I said, "has more important things to do. At least I hope so. Don't you agree?"

Rachel inclined her head.

"Jung has an explanation," I said. "Listen to this":

> The unborn work in the psyche of the artist is a force of nature that achieves its end either with tyrannical might or with the subtle cunning of nature herself, quite regardless of the personal fate of the man who is its vehicle. The creative urge lives and grows in him like a tree in the earth from which it draws its nourishment. We would do well, therefore, to think of the creative process as a living thing implanted in the human psyche.[89]

"God, nature, what's the difference?" asked Rachel.

"Wait, I didn't finish."

> In the language of analytical psychology this living thing is an *autonomous complex*. It is a split-off portion of the psyche, which leads a life of its own outside the hierarchy of consciousness. Depending on its energy charge, it may appear either as a mere disturbance of conscious activities or as a supraordinate authority which can harness the ego to its purpose.[90]

"Don't you see?" I said. "It's a complex that drives people to create. It's in the same category as collecting stamps or coins or match-book covers."

Rachel found that hard to swallow. "So artists are neurotic, is that it? Art is the result of neurosis?"

I gnashed my teeth.

"Dearest, you misunderstand the nature of a complex. It is a feeling-toned idea that gets you by the throat. It's only neurotic when it gets in the way of your life. You can be stimulated to create because of a complex, but what you produce still has to be shaped.

---

[89] "On the Relation of Analytical Psychology to Poetry," *The Spirit in Man, Art, and Literature,* CW 17, par. 115.

[90] Ibid.

You can't do that unless you have some distance from the complex. Granted, there are creative people who would do better work if they weren't neurotic. And there are neurotics whose creativity is locked in the closet of unconsciousness. Complexes are the key. Understand your complexes and it's a whole new ball game."

Rachel mused about that. "Where do I fit in?"

"You're the bridge to what's going on in me. You mediate the contents of my unconscious. Without you I'd have nothing to work with. Thanks to you, it wells up in me. It's all there, I can see it. But it has to be given an appropriate form. That's my job, alternately exciting and disheartening, and always threatened by the madness of the lead. Ms. Cotton Pants is a case in point."

Rachel snapped: "Well, now that you mention it, I haven't recovered from your writing on Ms. Cotton Pants. She wasn't my doing. I suppose you see her as a metaphor, but I was stunned by the sheer audacity of it. And what's the point of such prurience in a book that purports to be a serious appraisal of Jung's work?"

I shrugged. "I'm not sure, but perhaps to alert the reader to the shadowy reality behind the writer who is writing, a real person who is not just an automaton mouthing Jung. Once in a while, you know, I have an original thought."

"Still," said Rachel, "it is outrageous."

"I'll give you that," I replied. "Ms. Cotton Pants is an audacious conceit, but my account is symbolically true to what I know of the male psyche, and true too to my own enigmatic process of individuation. I will not gainsay myself. I like what I've made of Ms. Cotton Pants, so she stays. That's hubris, don't I know it, but what the hell, I'm just a pawn, after all. And you are so beautiful."

Rachel sniffed. "Now you stop that!"

I busied myself twisting paper clips into stick men while Rachel calmed down. I felt a bit uneasy because I was not used to opposing Rachel; usually I give way to her, not just to keep the peace but because she generally knows better.

"Okay," she said finally, "I think I get it. Ms. Cotton Pants is a complex of yours and you chose to play with it. But what starts the creative process? What sparks the complex?"

I leaned back. I could speak of archetypes, the collective unconscious; I could give examples from fairy tales, mythology and religion. I could cite literature from all over the world. Yes, like Jung I could babble on for a hundred pages and come back to square one.

"I don't know," I said. "It's a mystery to me."

Rachel smiled. "That's what I said in the first place—*God.*"

*

Jung did not write about American contemporary literary figures, but he emphatically did not appreciate the work of James Joyce. This was initially a surprise to me, for I thought Joyce gamboled in the symbolic, but Jung was not impressed:

> Joyce's *Ulysses,* very much unlike his ancient namesake, is a passive, merely perceiving consciousness, a mere eye, ear, nose, and mouth, a sensory nerve exposed without choice or check to the roaring, chaotic, lunatic cataract of psychic and physical happenings, and registering all this with almost photographic accuracy.
>
> *Ulysses* is a book that pours along for seven hundred and thirty-five pages, a stream of time seven hundred and thirty-five days long which all consist in one single and senseless day in the life of every man . . . . The stream begins in the void and ends in the void. . . . The pitiless stream rolls on without a break, and its velocity or viscosity increases in the last forty pages till it sweeps away even the punctuation marks. Here the suffocating emptiness becomes so unbearably tense that it reaches the bursting point. This utterly hopeless emptiness is the dominant tone of the whole book. It not only begins and ends in nothingness, it consists of nothing but nothingness. . . . As a piece of technical virtuosity it is a brilliant and hellish monster-birth.[91]

Well, that is quite a rant, which if nothing else might soothe the

---

[91] " 'Ulysses': A Monologue," Ibid., pars. 163f. Jung appends a caveat footnote: "My essay lacks not only any scientific but also any didactic intention, and is of interest to the reader only as a subjective confession."

troubled minds of those who never read more than Molly's erotic soliloquy at the end and thought they were missing something.

Jung's disdain for *Ulysses* is unrelenting,. Listen to this:

> You read and read and read and you pretend to understand what you read. Occasionally you drop through an air pocket into a new sentence, but once the proper degree of resignation has been reached you get accustomed to anything. Thus I read to page 135 with despair in my heart, falling deep asleep twice on the way. The incredible versatility of Joyce's style has a monotonous and hypnotic effect. Nothing comes to meet the reader, everything turns away from him, leaving him gaping after it. The book is always up and away, dissatisfied with itself, ironic, sardonic, virulent, contemptuous, sad, despairing, and bitter. It plays on the reader's sympathies to his own undoing unless sleep kindly intervenes and puts a stop to the drain of energy. . . . When I awoke quite a while later, my views had undergone such a clarification that I started to read the book backwards. This method proved as good as the usual one; the book can just as well be read backwards, for it has no back and no front, no top and no bottom. Everything could easily have happened before or might have happened afterwards. You can read any of the conversations just as pleasurably backwards, for you don't miss the point of the gags Every sentence is a gag, but taken together they make no point. . . . The whole book has the character of a worm cut in half, that can grow a new head or a new tail as required.
>
> The singular and uncanny characteristic of the Joycean mind shows that his work pertains to the class of cold-blooded animals and specifically to the worm family. If worms were gifted with literary powers they would write with the sympathetic nervous system for lack of a brain. I suspect that something of this kind has happened to Joyce, that we have here a case of visceral thinking with severe restriction of cerebral activity and its confinement to the perceptual processes.[92]

Talk about the madness of the lead! Clearly Jung was caught in a complex, and he knew it:

---

[92] Ibid., pars. 165f.

Yes, I admit I have been made a fool of. The book would not meet me half way, nothing in it made the least attempt to be agreeable, and this always gives the reader an irritating sense of inferiority. . . .

A therapist like myself is always practising therapy—even on himself. Irritation means: You haven't yet seen what's behind it. Consequently we should follow up our irritation and examine whatever it is we discover in our ill temper. I observe then: this solipsism, this contempt for the cultivated and intelligent member of the reading public who wants to understand, who is well-meaning and who tries to be kindly and just gets on my nerves. There we have it, the cold-blooded unrelatedness of his mind which seems to come from the saurian in him or from still lower regions—conversation in and with one's own intestines—a man of stone.[93]

And what of Joyce himself? Well, it is historical fact that James Joyce loved Switzerland and in the end was buried in Zurich, where a bronze statue marks the grave. It is also true that Joyce's daughter Lucia was certifiably schizophrenic and treated by Jung in 1934 at the Burgholzli Clinic. It is even reported by one of his biographers that Jung was instrumental in cutting off the monthly stipend gifted to Joyce by the wealthy Mrs. Edith Rockefeller McCormick.[94] And it is known that Joyce spent many years in crafting *Ulysses* before it was published, and it has since been hailed as a masterpiece.

Did Jung's personal bias for meaning in art miss the point of *Ulysses?* He wrote a conciliatory letter to Joyce in 1932, saying he found the book "a hard nut," and that he was "a perfect stranger who went astray in the labyrinth of your Ulysses and happened to get out of it again by sheer good luck."[95]

In spite of his personal reaction to *Ulysses,* Jung stops short of labeling Joyce or his work as pathological. His further comments in this essay reflect his attitude toward modern art in general, and cub-

---

[93] Ibid., pars. 167f. The acerbic tone of these remarks is rivaled by a recent comment to me by Jungian analyst Adam Brillig (ret.): "The only problem I have with Nietzsche is knowing where to put the 'z' in his name."

[94] Frank McLynn, *Carl Gustav Jung,* p. 324.

[95] Ibid., p. 325. The whole letter is reproduced in CW 15, pp. 133f.

ism in particular:

> It would never occur to me to class *Ulysses* as a product of schizo-
> phrenia. Moreover, nothing would be gained by that label, for we
> wish to know why *Ulysses* exerts such a powerful influence and not
> whether its author is a high-grade or a low-grade schizophrenic.
> *Ulysses* is no more a pathological product than modern art as a
> whole. It is "cubistic" in the deepest sense because it resolves the
> picture of reality into an immensely complex painting whose domi-
> nant note is the melancholy of abstract objectivity. Cubism is not a
> disease but a tendency to represent reality in a certain way—and that
> way may be grotesquely realistic or grotesquely abstract. The clini-
> cal picture of schizophrenia is a mere analogy in that the schizo-
> phrenic apparently has the same tendency to treat reality as if it were
> strange to him, or, conversely, to estrange himself from reality. With
> the schizophrenic the tendency usually has no recognizable purpose
> but is a symptom inevitably arising from the disintegration of the
> personality into fragmentary personalities (the autonomous com-
> plexes). In the modern artist it is not produced by any disease in the
> individual but is a collective manifestation of our time. . . . Just be-
> cause it is a collective phenomenon it bears identical fruit in the
> most widely separated realms, in painting as well as literature, in
> sculpture as well as architecture. It is, moreover, significant that one
> of the spiritual fathers of the modern movement—van Gogh—was
> actually schizophrenic.[96]

Still, Jung concedes that even modern art may be seen as a creative endeavor. Thus he damns it with faint praise:

> The distortion of beauty and meaning by grotesque objectivity or
> equally grotesque irreality is, in the insane, a consequence of the de-
> struction of the personality; in the artist it has a creative purpose. Far
> from his work being an expression of the destruction of his personal-
> ity, the modern artist finds the unity of his artistic personality in de-
> structiveness. The Mephistophelian perversion of sense into non-
> sense, of beauty into ugliness—in such an exasperating way that

---

[96] Ibid., par. 174.

nonsense almost makes sense and ugliness has a provocative beauty—is a creative achievement that has never been pushed to such extremes in the history of human culture.[97]

Then, after a brief review of the history of beauty in art from the beginning of the Christian era through the Baroque to the pre-Raphaelites, Jung finally says something about *Ulysses* that if not exactly complimentary is at least grudgingly admiring of the author's artistic intent:

> In its destruction of the criteria of beauty and meaning that have held till today, *Ulysses* accomplishes wonders. It insults all our conventional feelings, it brutally disappoints our expectations of sense and content, it thumbs its nose at all synthesis. . . . Everything abusive we can say about *Ulysses* bears witness to its peculiar quality, for our abuse springs from the resentment of the unmodern man who does not wish to see what the gods have graciously veiled from sight.[98]

Sound familiar? It's a little like the abused mate sticking around and asking to be hit again.

I think it is fair to say that it is the medievalism, the regressive nature, of modernism that so disturbs Jung. He sees its manifestations, of which *Ulysses* is but one, as "an almost universal 'restratification' of modern man who is in the process of shaking off a world that has become obsolete." And then a poke at his erstwhile friend and mentor: "They have this in common with Freudian theory, that they undermine with fanatical one-sidedness values that have already begun to crumble."[99]

Yes, the times were changing, and we are all heirs to that change, from a collective of believers to those who toil heartlessly at meaningless tasks and are more or less indifferent to the Mystery. The best one can say for our current times is that most of us have

---

[97] Ibid., par. 175.

[98] Ibid., par. 177.

[99] Ibid., par. 179.

shelter and enough to eat. At least in the West.

In the end, Jung is obliged to concede Joyce's creative talent, as well as his impact on the literary world, though he regrets it is in the service of destruction:

> One may safely call the book pessimistic even though at the very end, on nearly the final page, a redeeming light breaks wistfully through the clouds. This is only *one* page against seven hundred and thirty-four which were one and all born in Orcus [the Underworld]. Here and there, a fine crystal glitters in the black stream of mud, so that even the unmodern may realize that Joyce is an "artist" who knows his trade . . . and is even a past master at it, but a master who has piously renounced his powers in the name of a higher goal. Even in his "restratification" Joyce has remained a pious Catholic: his dynamite is expended chiefly upon churches and upon those psychic edifices which are begotten or influenced by churches. . . .
>
> . . . . There must be whole sections of the population that are so bound to their spiritual environment that nothing less than Joycean explosives are required to break through their hermetic isolation. I am convinced that this is so: we are still stuck in the Middle Ages up to the ears. And it is because Joyce's contemporaries are so riddled with medieval prejudices that such prophets of negation as he and Freud are needed to reveal to them the other side of reality.[100]

> It seems to me now that all that is negative in Joyce's work, all that is cold-blooded, bizarre and banal, grotesque and devilish, is a positive virtue for which it deserves praise. Joyce's inexpressibly rich and myriad-faceted language unfolds itself in passages that creep along tapeworm fashion, terribly boring and monotonous, but the very boredom and monotony of it attain an epic grandeur that makes the book a *Mahabharata* of the world's futility and squalor.[101]

Jung ends his essay by quoting Molly's lusty surrender—"and his heart was going like mad and yes I said yes I will yes"—and finally, a kind of wry tribute:

---

[100] Ibid., pars. 180f.

[101] Ibid., par. 191.

O *Ulysses,* you are truly a devotional book for the object-besotted, object-ridden white man! You are a spiritual exercise, an ascetic discipline, an agonizing ritual, an arcane procedure, eighteen alchemical alembics piled on top of one another, where amid acids, poisonous fumes, and fire and ice, the homunculus of a new universal consciousness is distilled![102]

*

For the record, I too find *Ulysses* unpalatable. But I feel the same way about the daily paper. There is so much death and destruction, doom and gloom, in the world today that sometimes I think the only alternative to immersing myself in Jung is to become a vegetable. I'd opt for avocado, but they tell me it's a fruit.

Now time for lucubrating, with MP on my mind and Natalie Cole in my ears:

> The very thought of you and I forget to do
> The little ordinary things that everyone ought to do
> I'm living in a kind of daydream
> I'm happy as a king
> And foolish though it may seem
> To me that's everything.
>
> The mere idea of you, the longing here for you
> You'll never know how slow the moments go till I'm near to you
> I see your face in every flower
> Your eyes in stars above
> It's just the thought of you
> The very thought of you, my love.[103]

---

[102] Ibid., par. 201.

[103] "The Very Thought of You." Lyrics by Ray Noble; Range Road Music, ASCAP.

16
Psychotherapy and a Philosophy of Life
(from *The Practice of Psychotherapy,* CW 16; vintage 1942)

Psychotherapy was at first simply an auxiliary method; only gradually did it free itself from the world of ideas represented by medical therapeutics and come to understand that its concern lay not merely with physiological but primarily with psychological principles. . . . Sooner or later it was bound to become clear that one cannot treat the psyche without touching on man and life as a whole, including the ultimate and deeper issues, any more than one can treat the sick body without regard to the totality of its functions.[104]

Instinct . . . always brings in its train archetypal contents of a spiritual nature, which are at once its foundation and its limitation. In other words, an instinct is always and inevitably coupled with something like a philosophy of life, however archaic, unclear, and hazy this may be. . . . Instinct cannot be freed without freeing the mind, just as mind divorced from instinct is condemned to futility. Not that the tie between mind and instinct is necessarily a harmonious one. On the contrary it is full of conflict and means suffering. Therefore the principle aim of psychotherapy is not to transport the patient to an impossible state of happiness, but to help him acquire steadfastness and philosophical patience in face of suffering. Life demands for its completion and fulfilment a balance between joy and sorrow.[105]

Jung's essay, then, is all about how you can appreciate yourself and life without necessarily becoming happier.

You are thirty, forty or fifty-something and sick at heart. You have a so-so job that pays the rent. You read the papers, listen to the

---

[104] "Psychotherapy and a Philosophy of Life," *The Practice of Psychotherapy,* CW 16, par. 175. This essay was the introductory address at the Conference for Psychology held in Zurich September 26, 1942.

[105] Ibid., par. 185.

radio, watch television, read self-help books and you still don't know what to believe or how to live. The environment is endangered, people all over the world are starving. Opposed religious forces are sharpening their knives. Closer to home, you are lonely, bored, fearful and anxious. You feel impotent. You have no energy and you cry a lot. You wonder if you're eating enough vegetables, too much meat or fat or salt, not enough fish or fiber, too much coffee, too may eggs? Every day you are confronted by new and disturbing discoveries in the fields of medicine and nutrition.

You wake up one morning thinking you just can't cope anymore, that one more day at the office will kill you. But you soldier on, one atom in the great collective molecule. You face the day with a brave front, but you are tired all the time. Somehow you make it through another day chasing deadlines and fall into a blessèd sleep. And then you dream:

> You are running and running, pursued by monsters, dragons, mobsters even. On and on, through ghettos, around corners, along dark streets. You end up in a back alley facing a high brick wall topped with barbed wire. There is no escape, you are trapped.

The wall is the limit of your endurance. You turn off the alarm, hide under the covers and wish the world would go away. You think of ending it all, but you haven't the means or the will.

It occurs to you to seek professional help—a shrink, a therapist, analyst, counselor, someone to talk to. You ask around and come up with some names.

First you see a psychiatrist. He listens to your woes and smiles. "You are suffering from a chemical imbalance." He gives you an assortment of pills. "Take a red one when you get up and before going to bed. The yellows are for when you feel glum in-between. Take a green if you feel suicidal, but do call my secretary before you take a purple. Good luck, keep in touch."

You take the reds and yellows and feel worse. You take a green and still feel like throwing yourself off a cliff. You dump the purples in the trash.

Next on your list is a Freudian analyst. "I can help," she says. She is attractive but her office is cold steel, impersonal. "It will take time, of course . . . childhood traumas, erotic conflicts, so on and so forth. I shall need to see you four times a week for at least five years. I trust you are a man of means."

The Adlerian psychologist is forcefully blunt. "You are small, you would like to be big. You have unconsciously arranged your life to have power over others. Be honest now, aren't some of your best friends tall?"

You see a cognitive therapist who is hearty and gives you some tests. "Your behavior is aberrant and your thinking is negative, but I can fix that. You need to learn some coping skills. Perhaps you are in the wrong occupation. Have you tried locksmithing? Ever thought of being a roofer?"

Finally, at your wits' end, you see an elderly woman who calls herself a Jungian. You never heard of that but she says it doesn't matter. She hears you out and shrugs.

"Modern life can be the pits," agrees Madam P. (as I shall call her), "but you don't have to take it lying down. I don't know what your problem is, but I believe you do. No one can find a cure for what ails you except you, and only you can identify it as a cure. You have many good years ahead of you. What do you want to do with them? Do you dream?"

Well now, you never thought of that before. Dream? Well, nightmares mostly.

Madam P. seems genuinely concerned. She speaks softly and listens closely. She reminds you of Ingrid Bergman and Katherine Hepburn or maybe Lee Remick. You recount your travails and the mess of your life. You long for a mate, someone to come home to, someone to love, share your life with. You hold nothing back, not even the fudging of your tax return.

Madam P. smiles. "I would like to work with you. Do you have the time and energy to find out who you are? Once a week would be enough. Are you interested in yourself?"

You skip out of that first session with new energy, new hope. You've drifted for years trying to please everyone but yourself and it hasn't worked. You've done what others wanted or needed. You seldom thought of yourself; that would be narcissistic.

Of course, that is only one possibility. There is no typical way to enter therapy, but when you're at the end of your tether you could do worse than see a Jungian analyst. They aren't plentiful, but if you dig a bit you could probably find one not too far away.

Madam P. gives you a book as you leave. At home you open it at random and read:

"Personally," said Adam, "I regard the existence of the unconscious as a fact so important and so topical that in my opinion it would be a great loss if its manifestations were to be found only in technical journals gathering dust in libraries. If ever there was a time when self-knowledge was the absolutely necessary and right thing, it is now. People are hungry for substance. They have no end of cake, but long for bread.

"Jung tells of an old peasant woman who wrote asking if she might see him just once. He invited her to come. She was very poor—intellectually too. She had not even finished primary school. She kept house for her brother; they ran a little newsstand. Jung asked her if she really understood his books which she said she had read. And she replied, 'Your books are not books, Herr Professor, they are bread.' "

Adam became thoughtful. "The world is in a God-awful mess," he said. "We are living in a time of great disruption. Political passions are aflame, internal upheavals have brought nations to the brink of chaos. So what else is new? The psychology of the individual is reflected in the psychology of the nation. Only a change in the attitude of individuals can initiate a change in the psychology of the nation.

"One of the great problems in our culture is that extraversion is overvalued. Introversion is generally viewed as a somewhat shady activity, if not downright selfish. Being active in the world is deemed to be the measure of one's worth. You don't become Citizen of the Year on account of the time you spend staring at the wall, and you don't get the Order of Merit for working on your dreams. Yet collective change involves first of all a change in oneself, which in turn requires an introspective system of accounting. And whoever gives careful consideration to personal life-events is bound to come up against the frontiers of the unconscious, which contains precisely what they need—bread, so to speak."[106]

Well, that's pretty heavy and it shakes you up. You return to Madam P. in a pensive mood. You tell her of your week and the dream of being trapped.

"You have a very serious disposition," she says. "Do you get out much? What do you do for social life, fun and adventure?"

You are shy by nature and can't bring yourself to join any of the online dating sites or go out to clubs, but there are some old friends who might respond.

> Hey Lucia, long time gone. What you doing these days? I think it could be fun to get together if you're available for coffee and a chat, or dinner even. I am free pretty much anytime, so suggest your pleasure if this interests you. Regards, Alvin.

You send a similar invitation to Veronica, once a fellow worker—but neither answers. Then one day you are shopping for new jeans at Banana Republic and you hit it off with the olive-skinned Iranian saleslady, name of Zahlia, who's around your own age. She outfits you with a smile, and on an impulse you ask if she would like to meet up with you after work. She considers a moment, then says Yes I will I will, yes.

Maybe a lonely soul to match your own. Never mind, it's a start, a possibility, and it animates you.

Psychotherapy in the short run is about becoming comfortable with your therapist and yourself as you know yourself to be, as opposed to what you pretend to others. In the long term it is about your psychological development from an unconscious clod to a sentient being aware of your strengths and limitations, and more in

---

[106] Daryl Sharp, *Living Jung: The Good and the Better,* p. 15.

charge of your life than you used to be.

One of Jung's basic beliefs, and arguably his most important message, is that the purpose of human life is to become conscious. "As far as we can discern," he writes in later life, "the sole purpose of human existence is to kindle a light in the darkness of mere being."[107] Part and parcel of this is achieving a balance, a right harmony, between mind and body, spirit and instinct. Go too far one way or the other and we become neurotic. Jung says it in one pithy sentence:

> Too much of the animal distorts the civilized man, too much civilization makes sick animals.[108]

The "civilized man" tends to live in his head. He prides himself on a rational approach to life, and rightly so. We are no longer apes. Thanks to reason, science and logic, instead of hanging from trees or living in them, we cut them down to build houses, which we then fill with appliances to make life easier—and they generally do except for the whimsical behavior of computers.

All the same, the more we lose touch with our other side, our instinctual base, the more likely it is that something will happen in us to bring about a proper balance. This is the basis for Jung's idea of compensation within the psyche. One way or another, we'll be brought down to earth. It is just when we think we have everything under control that we are most apt to fall on our face, and this is especially true when we don't reckon with the uncivilized, ten-million-year-old animal in us. Mercurius is waiting in the wings, not to mention the aliens.

That being said, unexamined instinctual behavior is a hallmark of unconsciousness and a fundamental characteristic of the undeveloped personality. Through analysis one can become conscious of the instincts and the many ways in which we are slaves to them.

---

[107] *Memories, Dreams, Reflections,* p. 326.

[108] "The Eros Theory," *Two Essays,* CW 7, par. 32.

But this is not done with a view to giving them boundless freedom. The aim is rather to incorporate them into a purposeful whole.

Jung defined consciousness as "the function or activity which maintains the relation of psychic contents to the ego."[109] In that way he distinguished it conceptually from the psyche itself, which is comprised of both consciousness and the unconscious. Also, although we may speak of ego-consciousness, in Jung's model the ego is not the same thing as consciousness; it is simply the dominant complex of the conscious mind. Of course, in practice we can only become aware of psychic contents by means of the ego; which is to say, the more we know about what's going on in our unconscious, the more conscious we become.

My analyst once said to me: "Think of what you've been, what you are now, and then reflect on what you could be." This is a useful exercise not only for a bird's-eye perspective on where you are on the journey of individuation, but also because it alerts you to what might be missing.

We live in a stream of events. Something new happens to us every day, but most of us are so caught up in routine that we don't even notice. Consciousness is the result of observing and reflecting on events instead of simply reacting to them. Routine especially gets in the way of being conscious. We can sleepwalk through life as long as we stick to the tried and true. I often get stuck in that mud myself and lose sight of other possibilities.

Becoming conscious primarily involves discriminating between opposites. As noted earlier, the basic opposites are ego-consciousness and the unconscious, so the first hurdle is to acknowledge that there are indeed some things about yourself that you're not aware of. Those who cannot do this are doomed forever to skim the surface of life. For those who can admit to another side of themselves, there is then the daunting task of discriminating between a whole range of other opposites—thinking and feeling, masculine and feminine, good and bad, and so on. And then there is the crucial

---

[109] "Definitions," *Psychological Types,* CW 6, par. 700.

difference between inner and outer, oneself and others; sorting that out can easily take a few years.

Jung describes two distinct ways in which consciousness is enlarged. One is during a moment of high emotional tension involving a situation in the outer world. We feel uneasy for no obvious reason, or strangely attracted to someone, and suddenly we understand what's going on. The other way is what happens in a state of quiet contemplation, where ideas pass before the mind's eye like dream-images. Suddenly there is a flash of association between two apparently disconnected and widely separated thoughts. In each case it is the discharge of energy-tension that produces consciousness. These sudden realizations and flashes of insight are what we commonly experience as revelations.

In Jung's model of the psyche, consciousness is a kind of super-structure based on the unconscious and arising out of it:

> Consciousness does not create itself—it wells up from unknown depths. In childhood it awakens gradually, and all through life it wakes each morning out of the depths of sleep from an unconscious condition. It is like a child that is born daily out of the primordial womb of the unconscious. . . . It is not only influenced by the unconscious but continually emerges out of it in the form of spontaneous ideas and sudden flashes of thought.[110]

Elsewhere he uses a different metaphor:

> In the child, consciousness rises out of the depths of unconscious psychic life, at first like separate islands, which gradually unite to form a "continent," a continuous land-mass of consciousness. Progressive mental development means, in effect, extension of consciousness.[111]

A child lives in a state of oneness with its primary care-giver. There is little separation between subject and object. As the grow-

---

[110] "The Psychology of Eastern Meditation," *Psychology and Religion*, CW 11, par. 935.

[111] "The Development of Personality," *The Development of Personality*, CW 17, par. 326.

ing child assimilates experience and develops personal bound-
aries—a sense of self separate from the outside world—so the ego
comes into being. There is a recognizable sense of personal identity,
an "I am." This goes on in fits and starts, until at some point you
have this metaphorical "land-mass of consciousness," surrounded
by the waters of the unconscious.

The first half of life generally involves this developmental process. If we get decent mirroring in the early years, we stand a good
chance of acquiring a healthy ego. But again, this is not the same
thing as being conscious. There are lots of take-charge people with
very healthy egos—captains of industry, politicians, artists, entre-
preneurs and so on—who are still quite unconscious. In fact this
would seem to be the rule rather than the exception. You can be a
leader, run things like a clock and manage others well. But if you
don't take the time to introspect, to question who you are without
your external trappings, you can't claim to be conscious.

Mature consciousness, according to Jung, is dependent on a
working relationship between a strong but flexible ego and the Self,
regulating center of the psyche. For that to happen one has to acknowledge that the ego is not in charge. This is not a natural process; it is *contra naturam,* against nature, a major shift in perspective, like the difference between thinking the earth is the center
of the solar system and then learning that the sun is. Bam! This
generally doesn't happen until later in life, when you look back on
your experience and realize there was more going on than you
knew. Ergo, something other than "you" was pulling the strings.

Becoming conscious, then, is not a one-time thing; it is a continuous process, *by* the ego, of assimilating what was previously
unknown *to* the ego. It involves a progressive understanding of why
we do what we do. And a major step is to become aware of the
many ways we are influenced by unconscious aspects of ourselves,
which is to say, our complexes.

Being conscious also has little to do with the accumulation of
knowledge or academic degrees. It is rather a function of how much

we know about ourselves. And although no one is ever totally unconscious, on the other hand we can only ever be relatively more conscious—compared to what we were before.

Jung visualized the unconscious as an ocean, because both are inexhaustible. Freud saw the unconscious, or subconscious, as little more than a garbage can of fantasies and emotions that were active when we were children and then were repressed or forgotten. Jung accepted that for awhile. He was an early champion of Freud's theories, but in the end Freud's vision just didn't accord with Jung's experience. Jung came to believe instead that the unconscious also includes contents we never knew were there: things about ourselves (in our personal unconscious), and then, at a deeper level (the collective unconscious), all the varied experiences of the human race, the stuff of myth and religion—a vast historical warehouse. Under the right circumstances, any of this can become conscious, and unconscious material is often straining to break into the light of day. Jung writes:

> Everything of which I know, but of which I am not at the moment thinking; everything of which I was once conscious but have now forgotten; everything perceived by my senses, but not noted by my conscious mind; everything which, involuntarily and without paying attention to it, I feel, think, remember, want, and do; all the future things that are taking shape in me and will sometime come to consciousness: all this is the content of the unconscious.[112]

And that is why, in spite of our best efforts, we will always be more or less unconscious.

To my mind, we are forever prisoners of our personal psychology, but if we work on ourselves enough we might make day parole. Or, to use the earlier metaphor, over time we can establish a few beachheads, but there are still all those other islands to consider as we develop a satisfactory philosophy of life.

*

---

[112] *The Structure and Dynamics of the Psyche,* CW 8, par. 382.

Well, some of the foregoing is not actually part of Jung's essay that is the subject of this chapter. However, I wanted to convey the gist of it in my own words. Now, here is Jung's final paragraph:

> The conference we are holding today proves that our psychotherapy has recognized its aim, which is to pay equal attention to the physio-logical and to the spiritual factor. Originating in natural science, it applied the objective, empirical methods of the latter to the phe-nomenology of the mind. Even if this should remain a mere attempt, the fact that the attempt has been made is of incalculable signifi-cance.[113]

*

By the way, just for the record, I invented Madam P. in the above account, and Alvin was in fact a tender charge of my own many years ago. I would enjoy writing of his colorful adventures with the beguiling Zahlia, who imbued his life with love and meaning, but I fear that would strain my relationship with Rachel beyond her gracious tolerance of Ms. Cotton Pants.

I am moved to add that fortunately, or not, in my experience women are generally tolerant of men's fantasies—unless they act on them, and then, if you'll pardon the expression, the shite hits the fan.

---

[113] "Psychotherapy and a Philosophy of Life," *The Practice of Psychotherapy,* CW 16, par. 191.

17
Marriage as a Psychological Relationship
(from *The Development of Personality*, CW 17; vintage 1925)

Whenever we speak of a "psychological relationship" we presuppose one that is *conscious*, for there is no such thing as a psychological relationship between two people who are in a state of unconsciousness. From the psychological point of view, they would be wholly without relationship. From any other point of view, the physiological for example, they could be regarded as related, but one could not call their relationship psychological.[114]

Marriage? Well, not only. This essay is about intimate relationships in general—how and why they work, why they don't.

Taking the above passage at face value, it is lamentably obvious that most relationships are not "psychological"; that is, they are not based on a deep and comprehensive understanding of oneself and others. Young men and women cleave to each other on the whole for instinctive gratification, not because they are enamored of the loved one's psychology. This may not be all bad, for at least it perpetuates the human race. But the truth is that the heart-felt words, "I love you," are generally motivated by physical desire, social standing and the like. All that is age-appropriate, and premarital talk of psychological verities and potential obstacles fall on ears deaf to what the lovers have not experienced. Jung says as much, pointing out the vast shadow areas still unknown to young men and women of marriageable age, areas of themselves that inevitably inform their choice of a mate, often to their later dismay.[115]

On the whole, depth psychology as it has been presented in these

---

[114] "Marriage as a Psychological Relationship," *The Development of Personality,* CW 17, par. 325.

[115] Ibid., pars. 327ff.

pages and the many books of others, is suitable more for older couples whose relationships have foundered, run aground, precisely because of the lack of the partners' self-knowledge. Even later education may not heal a broken relationship, but it can prepare both parties for another kick at the can, without blindfolds. After divorce or separation, they are indeed often ripe to know, and open to learn, about the role played by their respective psychologies—typology, projection, complexes, shadow, animus and anima—in their unhappy situation.

I am not suggesting that marriage counseling is the answer, or even individual therapy, though often it is. Truth to tell, becoming conscious is responsible for quite as many break-ups as kiss-and-make-ups. When projections are taken back, there is often nothing, or very little, to hold people together.

I once had a client, Wallace, who had started his own business when he was thirty-two years old. By the time he was fifty he had everything he'd ever dreamed of. He was respected and he could afford to do anything he wanted. At the pinnacle of his success, he gradually became aware that he was losing interest. Where he had passionately believed in what he was doing, now he began to doubt its value. Where he used to leap out of bed at dawn to greet the day, he started sleeping in till ten. Instead of promoting his products, pursuing new markets and so on—the kind of challenges he used to thrive on—he would chew a pencil and stare out the window, daydreaming. He looked at what he had created and found he had no energy for it. He continued to run things because he was afraid that without him the business would fall apart, but he resented it.

When he came to me he was anxious and very depressed. "I have a wonderful life," he said, and burst into tears.

Of course he didn't have a wonderful life at all. What he did have was a wonderful persona. Now it had cracked. It took six months in analysis for him to realize that. He kept coming back to this question; it plagued him no end: "When you have everything you want, what else is there?"

Wallace had no fantasies to speak of. He was a homebody, a family man through and through. He was comfortable with his wife and had no interest in other women. He was not active in playing or watching sports, and had no desire to travel to exotic places. Fast cars? He drove an old Ford pick-up and he couldn't see himself in anything else.

"It's embarrassing," he said, "I lack for nothing and I'm not happy. Why not?"

It is a lament I often hear from someone of that age. I have no ready answers. I know some theory and I've experienced my own process, that's all. His situation fit some patterns I'm familiar with, but he himself was unique. I trusted that his unconscious would come up with a resolution. If you pay attention, it usually responds. As Jung expresses such situations in this essay:

> Middle life is the moment of greatest unfolding, when a man still gives himself to his work with his whole strength and his whole will. But in this very moment evening is born, and the second half of life begins. Passion now changes her face and is called duty; "I want" becomes the inexorable "I must," and the turnings of the pathway that once brought surprise and discovery become dulled by custom.[116]

That describes almost exactly the feeling Wallace had. Of course it happens to women as well as men. It doesn't seem to matter whether they've lived a traditional lifestyle, where she was the homemaker and the man brought home the bacon, or if she had an active career of her own. Gender isn't a factor in a midlife crisis; it is a general and natural psychological event.

At some point people just run out of steam. They have dark thoughts and terrible moods. They don't have their former energy or ambition. Their outlook is bleak. In fact, they have all the symptoms of an acute neurosis, especially depression, which is typical in the transition from one stage of life to another.

---

[116] Ibid., par. 331a.

Few people think of themselves as neurotic But neurosis isn't a dirty word. Jung describes it simply as self-division, an inner state of disunity. "When you are not quite at one with yourself in a given matter," he says, "you are approaching a neurotic condition."[117] In terms of the Axiom of Maria, this is just the movement from one to two.[118] Once you were happy in the Garden, now you aren't. You have a conflict. You're caught between opposites and you don't know what to do. You are, in the Biblical phrase, "east of Eden."

Jung does not minimize the challenge and difficulties in becoming conscious. He pinpoints the middle period of life as one of enormous psychological importance:

> The child begins its psychological life within very narrow limits, inside the magic circle of the mother and the family. With progressive maturation it widens its horizon and its own sphere of influence; its hopes and intentions are directed to extending the scope of personal power and possessions; desire reaches out to the world in ever-widening range . . . . Thus man breathes his own life into things, until finally they begin to live of themselves and to multiply; and imperceptibly he is overgrown by them. Mothers are overtaken by their children, men by their creations, and what was originally brought into being only with labour and the greatest effort can no longer be held in check. First it was passion, then it became duty, and finally an intolerable burden, a vampire that battens on the life of its creator. . . . The wine has fermented and begins to settle and clear. . . . One begins to take stock, to see how one's life has developed up to this point. The real motivations are sought and real discoveries are made. The critical survey of himself and his fate enables a man to recognize his peculiarities. But these insights do not come to him easily; they are gained only through the severest shocks.[119]

Thus Jung sets the stage for the centerpiece of this essay, namely

---

[117] "The Tavistock Lectures," *The Symbolic Life,* CW 18, par. 383.

[118] See above, p. 51.

[119] "Marriage as a Psychological Relationship," *The Development of Personality,* CW 17, par. 331a.

a model of relationship, found nowhere else in his *Collected Works,* where one partner is contained by the other. Here is the pith of it:

> It is an almost regular occurrence for a woman to be wholly contained spiritually in her husband, and for a husband to be wholly contained, emotionally, in his wife. One could describe this as the problem of the "contained" and the "container."[120]

Note that "spiritually" is used here not in a religious sense, but rather to describe, in Jung's words, "a certain complexity of mind or nature, comparable to a gem with many facets as opposed to the simple cube."[121] He goes on to say that the more complicated nature (the so-called container, man or woman) has a tendency to dissociation—"the capacity to split off irreconcilable traits of character for considerable periods"—and so appear to be simpler than he or she actually is. Such a person, he adds, has "a peculiar charm."[122] This is as much as to say that your pig in a poke may turn out to be a weasel; that is, you may fall in love with a persona, but what you get is the whole hog. And what of the partner?—

> Adaptation to such natures, or their adaptation to simpler personalities, is always a problem. . . . Their partners can easily lose themselves in such a labyrinthine nature, finding in it such an abundance of possible experiences that their personal interests are completely absorbed, sometimes in a not very agreeable way, since their sole occupation then consists in tracking the other through all the twists and turns of his character. There is always so much experience available that the simpler personality is surrounded, if not actually swamped, by it; he is swallowed up in his more complex partner and cannot see his way out.[123]

---

[120] Ibid., par. 331c. Translator's note: "[In these passages] I have, for the sake of clarity, assumed that the container is the man and the contained the woman. This assumption is due entirely to the exigencies of English grammar, and is not implied in the German text. Needless to say, the situation could just as easily be reversed." (ibid., par. 333)

[121] Ibid., par. 331c.

[122] Ibid.

[123] Ibid.

Jung then describes the situation from the standpoint of the contained:

> The one who is contained feels himself to be living entirely within the confines of his marriage; his attitude to the marriage partner is undivided; outside the marriage there exist no essential obligations and no binding interests. . . . The great advantage lies in his own undividedness, and this is a factor not to be underrated in the psychic economy.[124]

Having a close relationship is nice and cozy. So far, so good. But there's a shadow side to that, as there is to everything—the possibility of discontent. It may not result in a search outside the relationship for someone or something else, but in what Jung goes on to describe as the contained person's "disquieting dependence" on the container:

> The unpleasant side of this otherwise ideal partnership is the disquieting dependence upon a personality that can never be seen in its entirety, and is therefore not altogether credible or dependable.[125]

The result is that the contained partner might feel insecure, have a nagging suspicion that what feels so good can't last. But that is not what is going on in the container-partner:

> The container, on the other hand, who in accordance with his tendency to dissociation has an especial need to unify himself in undivided love for another, will be left far behind in this effort, which is naturally very difficult for him, by the simpler personality. While he is seeking in the latter all the subtleties and complexities that would complement and correspond to his own facets, he is disturbing the other's simplicity. . . . And soon enough his partner, who in accordance with her simpler nature expects simple answers from him, will give him plenty to do by constellating his complexities with her everlasting insistence on simple answers. Willynilly, he must withdraw into himself before the suasions of simplicity. . . . The simpler na-

---

[124] Ibid., par. 332.
[125] Ibid.

ture works on the more complicated like a room that is too small, that does not allow him enough space. The complicated nature, on the other hand, gives the simpler one too many rooms with too much space, so that she never knows where she really belongs. So it comes about quite naturally that the more complicated contains the simpler.[126]

But that's not the half of it. Jung goes on like this:

Since the more complicated has perhaps a greater need of being contained than the other, he feels himself outside the marriage and accordingly always plays the problematical role. The more the contained clings, the more the container feels shut out of the relationship. The contained pushes into it by her clinging, and the more she pushes, the less the container is able to respond. He therefore tends to spy out of the window, no doubt unconsciously at first, but with the onset of middle age there awakens in him a more insistent longing for that unity and undividedness which is especially necessary to him on account of his dissociated nature. At this juncture things are apt to occur that bring the conflict to a head. He becomes conscious of the fact that he is seeking completion, seeking the contentedness and undividedness that have always been lacking. For the contained this is only a confirmation of the insecurity she has always felt so painfully; she discovers that in the rooms which apparently belonged to her there dwell other, unwished-for guests. The hope of security vanishes[127]

Jung's premise, then, is that the more complicated nature, the container, has an unconscious drive to be undivided in union with the other, while the contained one feels he or she has already found it, but is never quite sure. On both sides it is a matter of self-deception because of unconsciousness. In the search for personal completion (or call it love, why not), the projection of one's other half or soul-mate is bound to be a factor to some extent.

Togetherness. "One heart and one soul." That is the typical fan-

---

[126] Ibid., par. 333.
[127] Ibid.

tasy-thinking during courtship, and it can last even longer than the honeymoon. But as time goes on it becomes clear that life is not always what we want it to be. We are mere pawns in a psychological chess game. It often turns out that the contained one is not the match the container was looking for after all—he or she is *really* quite simple and uncomplicated—and the one who initially felt contained is in bed with a problematic container.

Thus Jung ups the ante in the quest for a harmonious relationship, one that can truly be termed "psychological" rather than instinctive. It is a tough row to hoe, no doubt about that. It is also clear, I trust, that the spiritual container and the emotionally contained can be of either gender; also that in any dynamic relationship the container and contained may change places under different circumstances over the course of time.

Incidentally, in case you wonder what happened to Wallace, my fifty-year-old entrepreneur, I can tell you it was one of my most successful cases. He finally went bankrupt! I call it a success because after a couple of years in analysis he realized where his energy wanted to go and he went with it. He said to hell with the business world, he wanted to make pots. He lost almost everything, sold his business for a pittance, but he turned his leaden life into gold.

Of course those close to him didn't see it that way. His wife, who had been quite happy in their symbiotic relationship, refused therapy and left him for someone else; his children thought he was crazy. But he could live with all that because he knew what he was doing and why. He felt fulfilled, satisfyingly engaged with his life, accepting all its ups, downs and loops.

18
The Symbolic Life
(from *The Symbolic Life,* CW 18; vintage 1939)

You see, man is in need of a symbolic life—badly in need. We only live banal, ordinary, rational or irrational things—which are naturally also within the scope of rationalism, otherwise you could not call them irrational. But we have no symbolic life. Where do we live symbolically? Nowhere, except where we participate in the ritual of life. But who, among the many, are really participating in the ritual of life? Very few.[128]

What is the "symbolic life"? What is meant by "symbolic thinking"? Why is it important and how do you do it? These are momentous questions with no simple answers.

Daily life is permeated with symbolic happenings that most of us tend to take literally because we know no better. How are we to learn, and who is there to teach us, the difference?

It is a fact that most of us lead mundane lives whose very banality precludes living symbolically. It is incumbent on us to get enough sleep in order to survive the next day—do our job, care for kids, shop for food and clothes, make meals, pay bills, read papers, write letters, etc., etc.—so it is understandable that we rarely find time to reflect on anything, let alone how we are influenced by our complexes. Indeed, the pace of modern life is such that most of us are neurotic, whether we know it or not. The wonder is that we can function at all, when just getting out of bed is the start of another heroic journey.

---

[128] "The Symbolic Life," *The Symbolic Life,* CW 18, par. 625. At this seminar talk to the Guild of Pastoral Psychology in London, Jung was asked first, if he foresaw a "next step in religious development," and second, his views on why believing Catholics were not as subject to neurosis as were Protestants. Jung replied that he was not as ambitious as the questions he was asked.

Okay, to return to the beginning, "What is symbolic thinking?" Well, let us start with what it is not: literal thinking. Say you had the following dream:

> I come home early from work and call to my wife. There is no answer. I mount the stairs and go into the bedroom. There she is on the bed, naked under Frank, my next-door neighbor, apparently enjoying herself. I fly into a rage and wake up.

How would you react to such an experience? The literal thinker, tied to equating inner images with outer reality, might jump out of bed and storm next door with a baseball bat to confront Frank: "You bastard! Stay away from my wife!"—as if what he saw in his dream had actually happened. Then might ensue an acrimonious physical fight with your happily-married neighbor, who had been trying to enjoy a morning coffee before running off to work, and moreover didn't even fancy your wife. But you never liked Frank anyway, so you are glad of the excuse to hurt him.

Symbolic thinking, however, would allow you to escape assault charges and ask yourself some cogent questions, such as, "What does my wife mean to me?" and "Who is the Frank in me that my wife is attracted to?" and "What is the difference between me and Frank?" Not to mention, "Is there something I can learn from my Frank shadow that might improve my relationship with my wife?"

Here's another example, from today's newspaper. An elderly man and an elderly woman are approaching each other on the sidewalk. They collide and neither will give way. They threaten each other with their canes. Her blows finally drive him off, but she is so angry that she sues the man. The court case goes her way and she feels vindicated, But psychologically she has lost, for she has not attended to the symbolic significance of the encounter. For instance, "What does this man represent to me?" or, "What is it about the masculine that threatens me?"

One could go on and on with examples from dreams and everyday life. The only trick to thinking symbolically is not to take dream images or what happens in daily life at face value. One needs to see what is behind the image or experience, what it is pointing to that is relevant to our process of individuation—who we are meant to be.

Symbolic thinking involves looking at the world sideways, not simply "out of the box," as corporate-think might have it, but quite "off the wall." It does not come naturally to me, though it seems to be second nature to some intuitives. I learned to think symbolically by immersing myself in Jung's writings (especially *Symbols of Transformation,* CW 5) and those of Marie-Louise von Franz, particularly her interpretations of fairy tales and arcane alchemical procedures. To this day, I don't know how to teach it; I can only say how I learned to become comfortable with it.

Jung believed that ritual was a great aid to symbolic thinking and a bastion against neurosis. He always maintained that religious rituals—especially those of the Catholic Church—saved many from becoming neurotic. In this essay he cites more than once the traditional mantra, "no salvation outside the Church." But he goes on then to point out that those who have lost their faith and are no longer contained in and protected by a dogmatic belief system, "no more in the lap of the All-compassionate Mother,"[129] are prime candidates for neurosis. Then, given the wherewithal, analysis is the only way to deal with their demons and self-division. Without a father-confessor, he thought, the only viable alternative was an analytic dialogue.

When we think symbolically, we tap into a layer of the psyche—the collective unconscious—that holds vast riches. Freud saw the unconscious as a repository of repressed childhood wishes and sexual fantasies. Then along came Jung, Freud's erstwhile star student, who said that wasn't the whole story, or even most of it.

Their differing views on neurosis was only the thin wedge of the schism between them. Jung's take on the unconscious, exemplified in his early masterpiece, *Symbols of Transformation,* estranged them irrevocably: Much later, in his autobiography, Jung wrote:

---

[129] "The Symbolic Life," *The Symbolic Life,* CW 18, par. 632.

Above all, Freud's attitude toward the spirit seemed to me highly questionable. Wherever, in a person or in a work of art, an expression of spirituality (in the intellectual, not the supernatural sense) came to light, he suspected it, and insinuated that it was repressed sexuality. Anything that could not be directly interpreted as sexuality he referred to as "psychosexuality." I protested that this hypothesis, carried to its logical conclusion, would lead to an annihilating judgment upon culture. Culture would then appear as a mere farce, the morbid consequence of repressed sexuality. "Yes," he assented, "so it is, and that is just a curse of fate against which we are powerless to contend." I was by no means disposed to agree.[130]

Now, before I came across Jung, I had studied Freud and found his work interesting, his writing style exemplary, but his perspective unsatisfying. However, Jung's approach to the psyche fed my soul and I embraced it. It is true that I have an enormous projection onto Jung as a man of exceptional wisdom, but it has served me well. I am awed by his greatness and proud to be one of his emissaries, so to speak, in company with the late great masters, Marie-Louise von Franz and Edward F. Edinger. Call it a Jung complex, fair enough; of course it is. But it's arguably more healthy than being obsessed with my golf score or net worth. Or as Sarah Vaughan sings in an appeal for Eros, "You can't keep me warm / with a racing form."[131]

It is worth repeating here what I wrote earlier:

A relationship, although it may be experimental, is not a scientific experiment, where you end up with a foreseen result—QED, it's called in Latin: *quod erat demonstrandum* (that which was to be proved). That was an important tenet in my early education, and for years I took that principle into life, but finally it just didn't work, and so no more. Logos has long since given way in my life to Eros. I no longer have to prove anything. I just have to honor how I feel, which as it happens is not really a whole lot easier than proving a

---

[130] *Memories, Dreams, Reflections,* pp. 149f.

[131] "Blue Grass," lyrics by De Sylva, Brown, Henderson.

hypothesis in physics. But I can tell you, it sure is more satisfying.[132]

Although elsewhere in his writings Jung is less than generous regarding the possibility of becoming conscious when contained in a religious dogma,[133] in this essay he is lavishly and explicitly admiring of the symbolism evidenced in rituals of the Catholic Church, which, he avers, saves many from becoming neurotic. Thus he writes:

> There is an old tradition in the Catholic Church of the *directeur de conscience*—a sort of leader of souls. These directors have an extraordinary amount of experience and training in that work, and I have often been amazed as the wisdom with which Jesuits and other Catholic priests advised their patients.
>
> Just recently it happened that a patient of mine, a woman of the nobility, who had a Jesuit father-confessor, discussed with him all the critical points of the analysis she made under my care. Of course, a number of things were not quite orthodox, and I was fully aware that there was a great conflict in her mind, and I advised her to discuss these matters with her father-confessor. . . . And then, after she had had that very frank talk, she told me all he said to her, and he had confirmed every word I had told her—a thing that was rather amazing to me, particularly from the mouth of a Jesuit. That opened my eyes to the extraordinary wisdom and culture of the Catholic *directeur de conscience*. And it explains to a certain extent why the practising Catholic would rather go to the priest.[134]

I was initially surprised to read this. Silly me, for of course it should not be surprising given Jung's appreciation of the healing potential of ritual, which pervades his work. He goes on:

> The fact is that there are relatively few neurotic Catholics, and yet they are living under the same conditions as we do. They are presumably suffering from the same social conditions and so on, and so

---

[132] *Jung Uncorked,* Book One, p. 36.

[133] See John P. Dourley, *The Illness That We Are: A Jungian Critique of Christianity.*

[134] "The Symbolic Life," *The Symbolic Life,* CW 18, pars. 613f.

one would expect a similar amount of neurosis. There must be something in the cult, in the actual religious practice, which explains the peculiar fact that there are fewer complexes, or that these complexes manifest themselves much less in Catholics than in other people. That something, besides confession, is really the cult itself. It is the Mass, for instance. The heart of the Mass contains a living mystery, and that is the thing that works. When I say "a living mystery," I mean nothing mysterious. I mean mystery in that sense which the word has always had—a *mysterium tremendum*. And the Mass is by no means the only mystery in the Catholic Church. There are other mysteries too. They begin with the very preparation of the baptismal water—the rite of the *benedictus fontis major,* or *minor* [blessing of the font], on the night of the Sabbath before Easter. There you can see that a part of the Eleusinian Mysteries is still performed.[135]

It should be acknowledged here that there are other religions which, when taken seriously, also provide a similar support. Deeply engaged Jews, Buddhists, Pagans, etc., may all experience a sense of the symbolic life through the rituals they practice. .

Jung goes on to compare our Western culture's attitude with that of primitive natives:

I once had a talk with the master of ceremonies of a tribe of Pueblo Indians, and he told me something very interesting. He said, "Yes, we are a small tribe, and these Americans, they want to interfere with our religion. They should not do it," he said, "because we are the sons of the Father, the sun. He who goes there" (pointing to the sun)—that is our Father. We must help him daily to rise over the horizon and to walk over heaven. And we don't do it for ourselves only: we do it for America, we do it for the whole world. And if these Americans interfere with our religion through their mission,

---

[135] Ibid., par. 615. The Eleusinian Mysteries were Greek rituals used to celebrate the mother goddess Demeter's descent into, and return from, the Underworld to rescue her daughter Persephone from the clutches of Hades. See Marion Woodman, *The Owl Was a Baker's Daguhter: Obesity, Anorexia Nervosa and the Repressed Feminine,* pp. 104ff.

they will see something. In ten years Father Sun won't rise any more, because we can't help him any more."[136]

Some might call that magical thinking, but Jung saw it as a truly religious attitude:

> Now, you may say, that is just a sort of mild madness. Not at all! These people have no problems. They have their daily life, their symbolic life. They get up in the morning with a feeling of their great and divine responsibility: they are the sons of the Sun, the Father, and their daily life is to help the Father over the horizon—not for themselves alone, but for the whole world.[137]

Mystery is soul-food. Symbols are mysterious; they fuel the imagination where reason and intellect are at sea. Take the notion of the virgin birth, prevalent in many religions other than Christianity.[138] Rational thought cannot understand it, but the soul accepts it as a psychological fact symbolic of spiritual conception. "We are not far enough advanced psychologically to understand the truth, the extraordinary truth, of ritual and dogma," writes Jung. "Therefore such dogma should never be submitted to any kind of criticism." He goes on:

> So, you see, if I treat a real Christian, a real Catholic, I always keep him down to the dogma, and say, "You stick to it! And if you begin to criticize it in any way intellectually, then I am going to analyse you, and then you are in the frying pan!" When a practicing Catholic comes to me, I say, "Did you confess this to your father-confessor?? Naturally he says, "No, he does not understand." "What in hell, then," I say, "did you confess?" "Oh, lousy little things of no importance"—but the main sins he never talked of. I have had quite a number of these Catholics—six. I was quite proud to have so many, and I said to them, "Now, you see, what you tell me here, this is really serious. You go now to your father-confessor and you con-

---

[136] "The Symbolic Life," *The Symbolic Life,* CW 18, par. 629.

[137] Ibid., par. 630.

[138] See Joseph Campbell, *The Mythic Image,* pp. 35, 62, 243, 246, 255.

fess, whether he understands or does not understand. That is of no concern. It must be told before God, and if you don't do it, you are out of the Church, and then analysis begins, and then things will get hot, so you are much better off in the lap of the Church." So, you see, I brought these people back into the Church, with the result that the Pope himself gave me a private blessing for having taught certain important Catholics the right way of confessing.[139]

And what of the Protestants? Jung is rather disdainful:

The splitting up of Prostestantism into new denominations—four hundred or more we have—is a sign of life. But, alas! It is not a very nice sign of life, in the sense of a church, because there is no dogma and there is no ritual. There is not the typical symbolic life.[140]

Overall, Jung clearly felt that people were much better off "in the lap of the Church," otherwise the only recourse for their psychic ills was analysis, a much hotter and harder row to hoe, and moreover a path for which not everyone is suited.

Now, it may be true that some people suffer from a chemical imbalance in the brain that can be treated with pills or other psychiatric tools—nor did Jung himself discount this possibility—but many more are just sick at heart, with lonely souls, because of the exigencies of life and lack of meaning. I think of some of my own clients—George, Wallace, Alvin, mentioned in earlier chapters—for whom the following remarks by Jung hit the nail on its very head:

You are alone and you are confronted with all the demons of hell. That is what people don't know. Then they say you have an anxiety neurosis, nocturnal fears, compulsions—I don't know what. Your soul has become lonely; it is *extra ecclesiam* [outside the Church] and in a state of no-salvation. And people don't know it. They think your condition is pathological, and every doctor helps them to believe it. . . . But it is neurotic talk when one says that this is a neurosis. As a matter of fact it is something quite different: it is the terrific

---

[139] "The Symbolic Life," *The Symbolic Life,* CW 18, par. 618.
[140] Ibid., par. 624.

fear of loneliness. It is the hallucination of loneliness, and it is loneliness that cannot be quenched by anything else. You can be a member of a society with a thousand members, and you are still alone.
That thing in you which should live is alone; nobody touches it, nobody knows it, you yourself don't know it; but it keeps on stirring, it
disturbs you, it makes you restless, and it gives you no peace.[141]

Speak to your inner others to assuage the loneliness. Give them
names, personalities. Listen to what they have to say. That is active
imagination and a good start to symbolic thinking.

*

I want to diverge here somewhat, without losing the point. In his
memorial tribute to Richard Wilhelm, the renowned Sinologist who
introduced him to *The Secret of the Golden Flower*, Jung refers to
what he calls "maternal intellect" as being the hallmark of a creative personality:

> As a rule the specialist's is a purely masculine mind, an intellect to
> which fecundity is an alien and unnatural process; it is therefore an
> especially ill-adapted tool for giving rebirth to a foreign spirit. But a
> larger mind bears the stamp of the feminine; it is endowed with a re-
> ceptive and fruitful womb which can reshape what is strange and
> give it a familiar form. Wilhelm possessed the rare gift of a maternal
> intellect.[142]

"Maternal intellect." Now, isn't that a radical concept to consider? Talk about symbolic thinking—this takes the cake. To culti-
vate a mind informed by both masculine and feminine? It is surely
something to aspire to, for it means the coming together of apparent
opposites—matter and spirit, Eros and Logos, even a melding of
directed and fantasy thinking.[143] Men, in their concretistic way,
tend to think of femininity as something filmily embodied in a
woman who cooks meals, does the laundry, cuddles the kids, and at

---

[141] Ibid., par. 632.

[142] "Richard Wilhelm: In Memoriam," *The Spirit in Man, Art, and Literature,* CW
15, par.76.

[143] See *Jung Uncorked,* Book 1, chap. 5, "Two Kinds of Thinking.".

the end of the day lies in bed waiting for her man. Well, it may be an enticing fantasy, but it is very far from lived reality.

Try asking a woman to create a ritual that symbolizes your relationship and see what you can learn. Men in general have to become wise to the reality of the women they mate with, which both derives from, and informs, the nature of their own inner woman, their soul. This is the work of a lifetime, and it can hardly succeed without thinking symbolically.

Consider this dialogue in a recent interview with the esteemed poet/painter/songwriter Leonard Cohen:

> "Have you learned a lot from women?"
> "Oh yeah. You learn everything from women."
> "Everything?"
> He leans in. "It is where you move into uncharted territory. . . .
>
> "The rest is just reinforcing wisdom or folly that you have inherited. But nobody can prepare anybody for an encounter with the opposite sex. Much has been written about it. You can read self-help books, but the actual confrontation as a young person with desire, this appetite for completion, well, that is the education."
>
> Cohen sits back in his chair, his ideas as well-worn and familiar as old sweaters. "Of course, women are the content of men and men are the content of women, and most people are dealing with this—whatever version of that longing there is. You know, of completion. It can be spiritual, romantic, erotic. Everybody is involved in that activity."[144]

Amen to that; we are all looking for completion. The problem is that we tend to seek it in the wrong places, in outer relationships instead of in encounters with our inner others.[145]

In that vein Jung speaks of the restless seeking of modern men and women:

> I met a woman in Central Africa who had come up alone in a car from Cape Town and wanted to go to Cairo. "What for?" I asked.

---

[144] Interview by Sarah Hampson, *Toronto Globe and Mail,* May 26, 2007.

[145] See James Hollis, *The Eden Project: In Search of the Magical Other.*

"What are you trying to do that for?" And I was amazed when I looked into her eyes—the eyes of a hunted, a cornered animal—seeking, seeking, always in the hope of something. I said, "What in the world are you seeking? What are you waiting for?, what are you hunting after?" She is nearly possessed; she is possessed by so many devils that chase her around. And why is she possessed? Because she does not live the life that makes sense. Hers is a life utterly, grotesquely banal, utterly poor, meaningless, with no point in it at all. . . . But if she could say, "I am the daughter of the Moon. Every night I must help the Moon, my Mother, over the horizon"—ah, that is something else! Then she lives, then her life makes sense, and makes sense in all continuity, and for the whole of humanity. That gives peace, when people feel that they are living the symbolic life, that they are actors in the divine drama. That gives the only meaning to human life; everything else is banal and you can dismiss it. A career, producing of children, are all *maya* [illusion] compared with that one thing, that your life is meaningful.[146]

*

My teenage sweetheart was a buxom blonde who dove and swam with the dolphins. We were mad about each other. We stripped our clothes off in my father's Desoto and played with each other—or toyed in the shadow of her father as we lay on the floor watching hockey games on television. She resisted intercourse. Fair enough, though I was crazy with desire. And after two years of intense, contained passion, she developed a thing for Paul Anka and I was toast. I didn't take it well. I was obsessed. I pestered her and wished she'd come back to me. So much for wallowing in lovelorn angst. No fun at the time, but a good lesson, in retrospect, of anima-possession. At that time I knew nothing of projection.

Now, in the twilight of my years, my calling is to draw attention to some psychological parameters for people young and old so they don't hurt themselves or others when they are inundated with frustrated feelings.

---

[146] "The Symbolic Life," *The Symbolic Life,* CW 18, par. 630.

But make no mistake about it—the kind of angst I experienced as a teenager can assail us at any age, even—or especially—when we are apparently conscious and know about the phenomenon of projection.

Here is Barbra Streisand, as a mature woman playing a teenage girl pretending to be a boy, on how a man makes her feel:

> There's no chill and yet I shiver
> There's no flame and yet I burn
> I'm not sure what I'm afraid of
> And yet I'm trembling
> There's no storm yet I hear thunder
> And I'm breathless why I wonder
> Weak one moment then the next I'm fine
>
> I'm a bundle of confusion
> Yet it has a strange appeal
> Did it all begin with him
> And the way he makes me feel
> I like the way he makes me feel, he makes me feel,
> I like the way, I like the way he makes me feel.[147]

Such poignant expressions of swirling emotional chaos! But she holds back; she doesn't say *what* makes her tremble; we can only imagine what "he" does to bring her feminine body and soul to life.

Lust is so mysterious. What is it about a particular man that excites a woman's passion when she is indifferent to others? You can find various answers in women's magazines and psychology journals—good looks, grooming, physique, intellect, social status, net worth, etc.—but they don't explain the improbable and seldom take note of projections and the influence of the unconscious.

Several women have told me they don't know why they respond lustfully to a man, but add that they don't have to know; they just feel it washing through them and let themselves enjoy it. Perhaps it is ineffable, beyond words. All in all, it would seem that a woman's

---

[147] "The Way He Makes Me Feel." From the film *Yentl;* lyrics by Streisand.

108 The Symbolic Life

desire is not activated by men in general. It is man-specific.

"Huh!" Rachel piped up. "If it's 'man-specific,' they know; they just aren't telling you."

Be that as it may, it is expressed by Eva Cassidy in this way:

> You are the one
> My heart goes crazy, crazy
> I can't explain
> It's just the way that you are
> You are the one.[148]

I think men's lust is more generic. A healthy male can become aroused at the sight of a pretty face, a head of hair, a shapely body. His desire is also less discriminating and tends to be less contained than a woman's; that is, he is inclined to want to make love to any woman who's willing. This is nothing for a man to be ashamed of. It is instinctive, archetypally programmed. Of course, a somewhat conscious man will be mindful of the potential consequences if he acts on his impulses. Between such a hammer and anvil is forged a personality of some substance.

Women generally take sexual activity more seriously. They tend to hope for a meaningful relationship, which is far from the average man's agenda when he takes a woman to bed. This is hardly news; I am just stating the obvious.

A stand-up comic, when asked what men want from a woman, replied, among other crude suggestions:

> Make egg sandwiches
> And not talk too much.

The traditional, patriarchal view is that a woman's place is in the kitchen and the bedroom. Well, it is clear that many men still feel that way, but any self-respecting man wants considerably more. Take me, I appreciate the beauty of a woman, but I make a mean egg sandwich myself, and only respond erotically to a woman who can hold an intelligent conversation, or maybe not.

---

[148] "You Are," lyrics by Tony Taylor.

*

I spend a fair amount of time staring at the wall. It keeps me sane in a crazy-making world teeming with random shootings, pollution, arcane diseases and internecine strife. On the blank wall I see my life writ large—past, present and potential future. I've had many insights staring at the wall, but of course it isn't always pleasant to be flooded by what I've done or left undone, or might yet do. And as often as not, the invisible writing on the wall tells me I am quite unworthy. As Franz Kafka expressed this feeling:

> At a certain point in self-knowledge when other circumstances favoring self-scrutiny are present, it will invariably follow that you find yourself execrable. . . . You will see that you are a rat's nest of miserable dissimulations.[149]

And this:

> At bottom I am an incapable ignorant person who if he had not been compelled to go to school would be fit only to crouch in a kennel, to leap out when food is offered him and to leap back when he has swallowed it.[150]

What gross images! Poor Kafka! Poor me! Now isn't that pathetic? Well, yes, but on the other hand, not really. In Jungian psychology we call it negative inflation, which erupts when we get too big for our boots; in other words, it is simply a manifestation of the self-regulating activity of the psyche, which kicks in to bring about a right balance, one way or the other. Take the feeling of worthlessness to heart, for sure, but don't be crushed by it, for the tide will turn. The Swiss folk-hero Til Eulenspiegel nailed it: he laughed when he was skiing uphill because he knew he'd soon be going downhill, and he cried when going downhill, foreseeing an imminent uphill climb. Just so, there is a natural, purposeful rhythm to our energy, and we had better get used to the ups and downs.[151]

---

[149] *The Diaries of Franz Kafka,, 1916-1923*, p. 114.

[150] *The Diaries of Franz Kafka, 1910-1913*, p. 308.

[151] Think *enantiodromia,* "the emergence of the unconscious opposite in the course

My life has been a patchwork quilt. Some patches have been my doing, some the work of others; some deliberate, some fortuitous. All in all, I cannot claim to be master of my fate. Looking back, it seems like I've been a hapless puppet, with someone or something else pulling the strings. Sometimes I feel like Captain Ahab chasing the great white whale. Sometimes I am Ishmael, sole survivor of a doomed voyage. Almost always I am at a loss. Though others may see me as a guru of sorts, staring at the wall reminds me that I am not. At best I am simply a fairy-tale Dummling in search of the treasure hard to attain. At worst, well never mind.

Such thoughts come to me on reading this essay by Jung. For that matter, virtually anything I read by Jung sets my soul on fire, prompts me to introspect and to think symbolically. I am Saturn-senex to the core, temperamentally and astrologically (Capricorn). I am faithful, focused and disciplined. I work hard. I am eminently responsible and conscientious. But my *sol niger* shadow keeps winking at me: "You are also fickle, lazy, unreliable, a cheat and a liar."

Well, those are the opposites I am obliged to live with. And who isn't, I'd like to know. But not everyone is aware of it or can stand the tension. No wonder people throw themselves off bridges or in front of trains. Better a quick end than an interminable internal battle. But that's not me. Although I tend to be pessimistic, I cling to the opposite, as does Frank Sinatra in this classic tune:

> Out of the tree of life, I just picked me a plum,
> You came along and everything started in to hum.
> Still it's a real good bet, the best is yet to come.
> The best is yet to come, and won't that be fine
> The best is yet to come, come the day that you're mine.[152]

I've already confessed to being an incurable romantic. So I'll continue to play ping-pong with life and MP. Maybe it helps to live

---

of time."

[152] "The Best Is Yet To Come," lyrics by Cy Coleman, Carolyn Leigh.

in a temperate climate, where bleak winters are inevitably followed by the new life of spring. There, now that's both literal and symbolic thinking, and here follows another rather fanciful example.

Time passes, yes, but who knows where it goes? Listen to Eva Cassidy on this theme:

> Across the evening sky
> All the birds are leaving
> But how can they know
> It's time for them to go?
> Before the winter fire
> I will still be dreaming
> I do not count the time
> For who knows where the time goes?
>
> Sad deserted shore
> Your fickle friends are leaving
> Ah, then you know
> It's time for them to go
> But I will still be here
> I have no thought of leaving
> You know I have no thought of time
> For who knows where the time goes? [153]

This brings to mind the poet Rainer Maria Rilke, who stretched his imagination to conceive of a neighbor, a Russian bureaucrat named Nikolai Kusmitch, who was obsessed with time.

Time was precious to Nikolai Kusmitch. He spent his days hoarding it, saving a second here, a minute or two there, sometimes a whole half hour. He imagined that the time he saved could be used to better advantage when he wasn't so busy. Perhaps it could even be tacked on at the end of his life, so he'd live longer.

He sought out what he thought must exist, a state institution for time, a kind of Time Bank you could make deposits in and then draw on. He didn't find one, so he kept the loose change in his head.

Nikolai Kusmitch did what he could to economize, but after a

---

[153] "Who Knows Where the Time Goes," Lyrics by Sandi Denny.

few weeks it struck him that he was still spending too much.

"I must retrench," he thought.

He rose earlier. He washed less thoroughly, ate his toast standing up and drank coffee on the run. But on Sundays, when he came to settle his accounts, he always found that nothing remained of his savings. He died as he had lived, a pauper.[154]

Working on yourself is something like that. You can't save it up for Sundays; it's what you do during the week that counts.

*

At the end of this seminar in which Jung delivered his views on Catholicism and the symbolic life, he said he believed that modern psychology was the future. He noted that he could not divine the historic future [this was 1939, and Nazi Germany was on the march], but the future he was concerned with was "the fulfilment of that will which is in every individual, My [future] history is only the history of those individuals who are going to fulfil their hypotheses"—that is, the movement toward individuation—

That is the whole problem; that is the problem of the true Pueblo: that I do today everything that is necessary so that my Father can rise over the horizon. That is my standpoint." [155]

There followed considerable discussion, during which Jung was asked, "What if a person can't find his way back to a church?"
Jung replied:

Then there is trouble; then he has to go on the Quest; then he has to find out what his soul says; then he has to go through the solitude of a land that is not created. I have published such an example in my lectures[156]—that of a great scientist, a very famous man, who lives today. He set out to see what the unconscious said to him, and it gave him a wonderful lead. That man got into order again because

---

[154] *The Notebook of Malte Laurids Brigge,* pp. 161ff (paraphrase).

[155] "The Symbolic Life," *The Symbolic Life,* CW 18, par. 639.

[156] See "Individual Dream Symbolism in Relation to Alchemy," *Psychology and Alchemy,* CW 12, pars. 44ff.

he gradually accepted the symbolic data, and now he leads the religious life, the life of the careful observer. Religion is careful observation of the data. He now observes all the things that are brought him by his dreams; that is his only guidance.[157]

I cannot gainsay that. I can only add that careful reflection on what is attentively observed is the hallmark of any psychological work on oneself. That can certainly be called a religious activity, though not in itself a religion.

To cap the seminar, Jung declares his seasoned view:

There is no conflict between religion and science. That is a very old-fashioned idea. Science has to consider what there is. There is religion, and it is one of the most essential manifestations of the human mind. It is a fact, and science has nothing to say about it; it simply has to confirm that there is that fact. Science always runs after these things; it does not try to explain the phenomena. Science cannot establish a religious truth. A religious truth is essentially an experience, it is not an opinion. Religion is an absolute experience. A religious experience is absolute, it cannot be discussed. For instance, when somebody has had a religious experience, he just has such an experience, and nothing can take it away from him.[158]

So endeth this lesson, symbolically, but literally grounded.

---

[157] *The Symbolic Life,* CW 18, par. 673. We now know that the scientist mentioned was Wolfgang Pauli, Nobel Laureat in physics. See J. Gary Sparks, *At the Heart of Matter,* for an authoritative discussion of Pauli's contribution to Jung's ideas on synchronicity and the helpful collaboration of Marie-Louise von Franz.

[158] Ibid., par. 692. See also Edward F. Edinger, *The Creation of Consciousness,* pp. 57ff. for a lengthier psychological commentary on science and religion.

Afterword

It was not easy to choose which of Jung's essays to write about in this book. Jung's *Collected Works* are such a cornucopia. As an inveterate "classical Jungian," I believe that everything he wrote deserves close attention.

My choices, then, have been somewhat arbitrary and entirely subjective. I can only hope that they find some favor with readers and stimulate them to go to the sources for further enlightenment on the significance and importance of analytical psychology today.

*

This concludes Book Two of *Jung Uncorked*. Book One, published separately, explicates and comments on essays from Jung's *Collected Works* volumes CW 1 *(Psychiatric Studies)* to CW 9i *(The Archetypes and the Collective Unconscious)*. It has its own bibliography and index.

.

Bibliography

Adler, Alfred. *The Individual Psychology of Alfred Adler*. Ed. Heinz Ansbacher and Rowena Ansbacher. New York: Basic Books, 1956.

Bulfinch, Thomas. *Bulfinch's Mythology: The Age of Fable*. Garden City, NY: Doubleday & Company, 1968.

Campbell, Joseph. *The Mythic Image* (Bollingen Series C). Assisted by M.J. Abadie. Princeton: Princeton University Press, 1974.

Carotenuto, Aldo. *Eros and Pathos: Shades of Love and Suffering*. Toronto: Inner City Books, 1989.

de Vries, Ad. *Dictionary of Imagery and Symbolism*. Amsterdam: North-Holland Publishing Co., 1974.

Dostoyevsky, Fyodor. *Notes from Underground*. Trans. Andrew McAndrew. New York: Signet, 1961.

Dourley, John P. *The Illness That We Are: A Jungian Critique of Christianity*. Toronto: Inner City Books, 1984.

_____. *A Strategy for a Loss of Faith*. Toronto: Inner City Books, 1992

Edinger, Edward F. *Anatomy of the Psyche: Alchemical Symbolism in Psychotherapy*. La Salle, IL: Open Court, 1985.

_____. *The Aion Lectures: Exploring the Self in Jung's* Aion. Toronto: Inner City Books, 1996.

_____. *The Creation of Consciousness: Jung's Myth for Modern Man*. Toronto: Inner City Books, 1984.

_____. *Encounter with the Self: A Jungian Commentary on William Blake's Illustrations of the Book of Job*. Toronto: Inner City Books, 1986.

_____. *The Mysterium Lectures: A Journey Through Jung's* Mysterium Coniunctionis. Toronto: Inner City Books, 1995.

_____. *The Mystery of the Coniunctio: Alchemical Image of Individuation*. Toronto: Inner City Books, 1994.

_____. *Science of the Soul: A Jungian Perspective*. Toronto: Inner City Books, 2002.

_____. *Transformation of the God-Image: An Elucidation of Jung's "Answer to Job."* Toronto: Inner City Books, 1992.

Freud, Sigmund. *The Complete Psychological Works of Sigmund Freud.* Ed. James Strachey. London, UK: The Hogarth Press, 1978.

Frey-Rohn, Liliane. *From Freud to Jung: A Comparative Study of the Psychology of the Unconscious.* Boston: Shambhala Publications, 1974.

Grimm Brothers. *Complete Grimm's Fairy Tales.* New York: Pantheon Books, 1944.

Hannah, Barbara. *Jung: His Life and Work (A Biographical Memoir).* New York: Capricorn Books, G.P. Putnam's Sons, 1976.

Harding, M. Esther. *The Way of All Women: A Psychological Interpretation.* London, UK: Rider & Company, 1971.

Hillman, James. *Loose Ends.* Zurich: Spring Publications, 1975.

_____. *The Myth of Analysis: Three Essays in Archetypal Psychology.* Evanston, IL.: Northwestern University Press, 1972.

Hollis, James. *The Middle Passage: From Misery to Meaning in Midlife.* Toronto: Inner City Books, 1993.

_____. *The Eden Project: In Search of the Magical Other.* Toronto: Inner City Books, 1998.

Jacoby, Mario. *Longing for Paradise: Psychological Perspectives on an Archetype.* Toronto: Inner City Books, 2006.

Jaffe, Lawrence W. *Liberating the Heart: Spirituality and Jungian Psychology.* Toronto: Inner City Books, 1990.

Janouch, Gustav. *Conversations with Kafka.* Trans. Goronwy Rees. 2nd edition, revised and enlarged. London, UK: Andre Deutsch, 1971.

Jung, C.G. *C.G. Jung Letters.* (Bollingen Series XCV). 2 vols. Ed. Gerhard Adler and Aniela Jaffé. Princeton: Princeton University Press, 1973.

_____. *The Collected Works of C.G. Jung* (Bollingen Series XX). 20 vols. Trans. R.F.C. Hull. Ed. H. Read, M. Fordham, G. Adler, Wm. McGuire. Princeton: Princeton University Press, 1953-1979.

_____. *Memories, Dreams, Reflections.* Ed. Aniela Jaffé. New York: Pantheon Books, 1961.

Jung, Carl G., and von Franz, Marie-Louise, eds. *Man and His Symbols.* London, UK: Aldus Books, 1964.

Kafka, Franz. *The Diaries of Franz Kafka,, 1910-1913.* Trans. Joseph Kresh. Ed. Max Brod. London, UK: Secker & Warburg, 1948.

_____. *The Diaries of Franz Kafka,, 1916-1923.* Trans. Martin Greenberg and Hannah Arendt. Ed. Max Brod. London, UK: Secker & Warburg, 1949.

_____. *The Penal Colony: Stories and Short Pieces.* Trans. Willa and Edwin Muir. New York: Schocken Books, 1961.

McGuire, William, ed. *The Freud/Jung Letters* (Bollingen Series XCIV). Trans. Ralph Manheim and R.F.C. Hull. Princeton: Princeton University Press, 1974.

McGuire, William, and Hull, R.F.C., eds. *C.G. Jung Speaking: Interviews and Encounters* (Bollingen Series XCVII. Princeton: Princeton University Press, 1977.

McLynn, Frank. *Carl Gustav Jung.* New York: St. Martin's Griffin Press, 1996.

Onians, R.B. *The Origins of European Thought.* Cambridge, MA: Cambridge University Press, 1951.

Perera, Sylvia Brinton. *Descent to the Goddess: A Way of Initiation for Women.* Toronto: Inner City Books, 1981.

Qualls-Corbett, Nancy. *The Sacred Prostitute: Eternal Aspect of the Feminine.* Toronto: Inner City Books, 1988.

Rank, Otto. *The Trauma of Birth.* New York: Robert Brunner, 1952.

Rilke, Rainer Maria. *R,M, Rilke: The Duino Elegies.* Trans. Stephen Garmey and Jay Wilson, New York: Harper & Row, 1972.

_____. *The Notebooks of Malte Laurids Brigge.* Trans. John Linton. London, UK: The Hogarth Press, 1959.

Sharp, Daryl. *Chicken Little: The Inside Story (a Jungian romance).* Toronto: Inner City Books, 1993.

_____. *Dear Gladys: The Survival Papers, Book. 2.* Toronto: Inner City Books, 1989.

_____. *Eyes Wide Open: Late Thoughts (a Jungian romance).* Toronto:

Inner City Books, 2007.

_____. *Jung Lexicon: A Primer of Terms and Concepts.* Toronto: Inner City Books, 1991.

_____. *Jung Uncorked: Rare Vintages from the Cellar of Analytical Psychology.* 2 vols. Toronto: Inner City Books, 2008.

_____. *Jungian Psychology Unplugged: My Life as an Elephant.* Toronto, Inner City Books, 1998.

_____. *Living Jung: The Good and the Better.* Toronto: Inner City Books, 1996.

_____. *Not the Big Sleep: On Having Fun, Seriously (a Jungian romance).* Toronto: Inner City Books, 2005.

_____. *On Staying Awake: Getting Older and Bolder (another Jungian romance). Toronto: Inner City Books, 2006.*

_____. *Personality Types: Jung's Model of Typology.* Toronto: Inner City Books, 1987.

_____. *The Secret Raven: Conflict and Transformation in the Life of Franz Kafka.* Toronto: Inner City Books, 1980.

_____. *The Survival Papers: Anatomy of a Midlife Crisis.* Toronto: Inner City Books, 1988.

_____. *Who Am I, Really? Personality, Soul and Individuation.* Toronto: Inner City Books, 1995.

Sparks, J. Gary. *At the Heart of Matter: Synchronicity and Jung's Spiritual Testament.* Toronto: Inner City Books, 2007

Stevens, Anthony. *Archetype Revisited: An Updated Natural History of the Self.* Toronto: Inner City Books, 2003.

von Franz, Marie-Louise. *Alchemy: An Introduction to the Symbolism and the Psychology.* Toronto: Inner City Books, 1980.

_____. *Animus and Anima in Fairy Tales.* Toronto: Inner City Books, 2002.

_____. *On Dreams and Death: A Jungian Interpretation.* Revised ed. with Foreword by Emmanuel Kennedy-Xipolitas. Trans. Emmanuel Kennedy-Xipolitas and Vernon Brooks. La Salle, IL.: Open Court, 1998.

_____. *C.G. Jung: His Myth in Our Time.* Toronto: Inner City Books, 1998.

_____. *The Interpretation of Fairy Tales.* Zurich: Spring Publications, 1973.

_____. *On Divination and Synchronicity.* Toronto: Inner City Books, 1980.

_____. *The Problem of the Puer Aeternus.* Toronto: Inner City Books, 2000.

_____. *A Psychological Interpretation of the Golden Ass of Apuleius: The Liberation of the Feminine in Man.* Revised ed. Boston: Shambhala Publications, 1992.

_____. *Redemption Motifs in Fairy Tales.* Toronto: Inner City Books, 1980.

Von Franz, Marie-Louise, ed. with commentary. *Aurora Consurgens: A Document Attributed to Thomas Aquinas on the Problem of Opposites in Alchemy.* Toronto: Inner City Books, 2000.

Von Franz, Marie-Louise, and Hillman, James. *Jung's Typology.* New York: Spring Publications, 1971.

Woodman, Marion. *Addiction to Perfection: The Still Unravished Bride.* Toronto: Inner City Books, 1982

_____. *Conscious Femininity: Interviews with Marion Woodman.* Toronto: Inner City Books, 1993.

_____. *The Owl Was a Baker's Daughter: Obesity, Anorexia Nervosa and the Repressed Feminine.* Toronto: Inner City Books, 1980.

_____. *The Pregnant Virgin: A Process of Psychological Transformation.* Toronto: Inner City Books, 1985.

Index

Entries in *italics* refer to illustrations

Also by Daryl Sharp in this Series

Please see last page for discounts and postage/handling.

THE SECRET RAVEN
Conflict and Transformation in the Life of Franz Kafka
ISBN 978-0-919123-00-7. (1980) 128 pp. $25

PERSONALITY TYPES: Jung's Model of Typology
ISBN 978-0-919123-30-9. (1987) 128 pp. **Diagrams** $25

THE SURVIVAL PAPERS: Anatomy of a Midlife Crisis
ISBN 978-0-919123-34-2. (1988) 160 pp. $25

DEAR GLADYS: The Survival Papers, Book 2
ISBN 978-0-919123-36-6. (1989) 144 pp. $25

JUNG LEXICON: A Primer of Terms and Concepts
ISBN 978-0-919123-48-9. (1991) 160 pp. **Diagrams** $25

GETTING TO KNOW YOU: The Inside Out of Relationship
ISBN 978-0-919123-56-4. (1992) 128 pp. $25

THE BRILLIG TRILOGY:

1. CHICKEN LITTLE: The Inside Story *(A Jungian romance)*
ISBN 978-0-919123-62-5. (1993) 128 pp. $25

2. WHO AM I, REALLY? Personality, Soul and Individuation
ISBN 978-0-919123-68-7. (1995) 144 pp. $25

3. LIVING JUNG: The Good and the Better
ISBN 978-0-919123-73-1. (1996) 128 pp. $25

JUNGIAN PSYCHOLOGY UNPLUGGED: My Life as an Elephant
ISBN 978-0-919123-81-6. (1998) 160 pp. $25

DIGESTING JUNG: Food for the Journey
ISBN 978-0-919123-96-0. (2001) 128 pp. $25

JUNG UNCORKED: Rare Vintages from the Cellar of Analytical Psychology
Two books. ISBN 978-1-894574-21-1/22-8.. (2008) 128 pp. each. $25 each

THE SLEEPNOT TRILOGY:

1. NOT THE BIG SLEEP: On having fun, seriously *(A Jungian romance)*
ISBN 978-0-894574-13-6. (2005) 128 pp. $25

2. ON STAYING AWAKE: Getting Older and Bolder *(Another Jungian romance)*
ISBN 978-0-894574-16-7. (2006) 144 pp. $25

3. EYES WIDE OPEN: Late Thoughts *(Another Jungian romance)*
ISBN 978-0-894574-18-1.. (2007) 160 pp. $25